Expressions of Love

Woman's Day®
Prizewinning
Cross-Stitch Samplers

Theresa Capuana, Needlework and Crafts Editor,
Woman's Day®
Helen Donnally, Editor

Sedgewood® Press

New York

Acknowledgments

The "Expressions of Love" contest was cosponsored by
Woman's Day and The National Needlework Association
(TNNA). This association, headquartered in New York
City, is a nonprofit trade association that was established
in 1975 to foster greater understanding and consumer aware-
ness of the needle arts of knitting, crocheting, canvas
work and embroidery. Its membership includes over a
thousand manufacturers, importers, distributors and
retailers. TNNA sponsors ongoing educational and pub-
licity programs, including national design contests.

For Diamandis Communications Inc.

Editorial Director: *Geraldine Rhoads*
Needlework and Crafts Editor: *Theresa Capuana*
Project Editor: *Helen Donnally*
Illustrator: *Roberta Frauwirth*
Photographer: *Ben Calvo*
Stylist: *Lina Morielli*

For Sedgewood® Press

Director: *Elizabeth P. Rice*
Editorial Project Manager: *Barbara Machtiger*
Project Editor: *Sandy Towers*
Production Manager: *Bill Rose*
Designer: *Diane Wagner*

Contents

General Directions

Dear Crafter:

We're delighted that you have in your hands *Expressions of Love: Woman's Day® Prizewinning Cross-Stitch Samplers*. The beautiful samplers you'll find inside are the winners in *Woman's Day*'s Expressions of Love cross-stitch contest. They were designed and executed by needleworkers throughout the country who share a love of cross-stitch. Whether you use these designs as they are shown here or choose to take a part of one or several, we are sure that you will be inspired to create your own handcrafted expressions of love.

This book is one of many published to date by Sedgewood® Press (and we have many more planned for the future). Sedgewood, begun in 1982, exists in order to bring you high-quality books with fine designs, both traditional and unusual uses for projects, clear instructions, and full color throughout, with every project shown in a color photograph.

Proud as we may be of our books, though, the real proof of their success is in the doing. We hope you will enjoy *Expressions of Love*, will use it happily to create your own personal samplers, and will look forward to the publication of more Sedgewood titles.

Sincerely,

Elizabeth P. Rice
Director, Sedgewood® Press

Introduction

Needlework is seen as a womanly art, even though some men find stitching a beautiful piece no less manly than working with leather or fitting a model ship with tiny sails. In fact, some of our contestants hail from families in which husbands and fathers boast of their needleworking skills.

But embroidery has been a principal creative outlet for women throughout history. Fabric has been the canvas and needles the tools with which women have celebrated and visually preserved the occasions, emotions, and symbols that constitute our heritage. It is in this work that they have recorded the historic events as well as the everyday happenings of their lives. The Bayeaux tapestry, for example, a work predating the printing press, is the only record of certain events that occurred during the Norman Conquest of England from 1066 to 1072.

The embroidered sampler dates back to before Shakespeare. Helena talks about her sampler in *A Midsummer Night's Dream,* and Milton refers to a sampler in *Comus.*

But European samplers of this antiquity were pattern books, in effect: embroideries done to record stitches and patterns the needleworker had mastered. Long and narrow, they could be rolled up for storage and consulted when needed. The first American samplers were of this sort, too, like the one by Loara Standish, Captain Myles Standish's daughter, which is now in Pilgrim Hall in Plymouth, Massachusetts.

The samplers that most beguile us today are the work of 18th- and 19th-century schoolgirls for whom they were exercises in stitchery. They learned embroidery not only at home but also in dame schools teaching reading, writing—and sewing. Stitching the alphabet effectively taught little girls their ABCs, and also made them proficient in marking household linens. Some of their teachers thought inspiring sayings, like Bible quotations, were educational, so you will find many early samplers featuring these.

Some young ladies of means later went on to academies, where they progressed to the study of academic subjects, dancing and manners, as well as more elaborate fancywork. Their samplers were frequently framed and displayed to show off their mastery of household arts.

Schoolgirl samplers continue to be most prized by needlework collectors. In fact, the sale of a 1788 sampler worked by Ruthy Rogers, a Marblehead, Massachusetts, 10-year-old, set the world record for needlework prices in 1987. Her embroidery picturing a girl, a tree, flowers and two birds brought $198,000 at auction.

Most sampler collections on view around the country are confined to pieces worked before the mid-1800s. After the Revolutionary War, silk from China had become more available, and there was a vogue for painting on silk. Deeper into the century, the Victorians turned to Berlin work, for which the German originators supplied printed patterns. How much easier it was to work with printed patterns! The woman's magazine, too, came into its own in the second half of the 1800s, offering printed needle-work instructions for readers. Schools ceased to emphasize instruction in sewing and, by the 20th century, embroidery was the pastime of adult women, much of it executed with the aid of printed patterns, transfers, and stamped goods.

Counted cross-stitch, with its open invitation to embroiderers to create decorative pictures, did not become popular in America again until the late 1960s and early 1970s. So the samplers in our contest are much more akin to early American work, in that they express the designers' own feelings and reflect their individual lives, rather than the copied needle-work stitched by our mothers, grandmothers, and even great- and great-great-grandmothers. As one of our contest judges noted, these samplers aren't cookie-cutter copies of other people's sentiments and experiences.

The winning designers remind us that many of today's families are spread apart, and they feel a need for closer connections. Their children could not be more loved, yet clearly a lot of tolerance has to be built into love when you have bright, restless little ones. Many of the designers see cross-stitch as a soothing pastime on days when children are obstreperous.

At least half of our prizewinners favor cross-stitch because it is portable and relaxing. This is as true of professional designers as of beginners, although few of our entrants were at either extreme. Most had some cross-stitch experience, and sometimes a long involvement with other needlework or crafts, but offered their very first original designs in the "Expressions of Love" competition. Most of our needleworkers make pieces for themselves or for friends—and stitch away for pure pleasure.

Our contestants wrote remarkable letters. Clearly they have a great feeling for words, thoughts, and ideas. They are also very busy women. A typical letter tells us of a schedule that eats up virtually every minute of the day . . . then explains how calming it is to squeeze out time for a sampler after the children are asleep, while waiting at the doctor's or dentist's office or watching over kids at the pool or filling in a few minutes during an office lunch break. One contestant gives thanks for having the contest project to keep her occupied when she was abstaining from drinking. There are a number of military and other much-traveled families represented here: These entrants found cross-stitching a soothing occupation on long trips.

Cross-stitching proves even more engrossing when a brand-new idea takes shape, and we hope this book will encourage both the experienced needleworker and those new to the pleasures of stitchery to experience for themselves the adventure of creating an original sampler.

How to Get the Most Pleasure from This Book

As our prizewinning designers have advised us, their work occupied them for varying periods of time—only a day, in the case of Shanon Allen's piece, more like a year for the sampler in which Nancy Roberts expresses her joy in the things that give her spiritual contentment. (Hers was the largest sampler in the winning group.)

In between there are designs offering great variety in their complexity. *Just choose what suits you:* a project that can be stitched in spare moments, here and there, and finished quickly, or one that will be a source of continuing pleasure as you work it for a long stretch of time.

There is also in this volume a treasury of ideas to stimulate your own creativity, and we hope you will mine the book for alphabets, motifs, and other design components to help you develop original samplers.

You have a wide choice of alphabets. We have included eleven alphabets, as well as seven number series, enabling you to plot many samplers of your own—with any sayings that delight you, the names of any dear ones you want to honor and, of course, any dates you want to commemorate. (Use these also to initial and date your work.) Some of the alphabets incorporate flowers, such as the one by Nancy Roberts; some are old-fashioned; some are contemporary.

There are borders galore: Florals such as Lin Vickery's, a lacy backstitch border by Laura Jourdan, scallops such as Evonne Cano's, patchwork squares such as Marylynn Cormier's, hearts and flowers such as Kerry Higginbotham's, couched ribbons as in Karen Montgomery's, the geometric ribbon border so effectively framing Bonnie Patterson's old-fashioned sampler, the tender little vines in Janet Newland's, an alphabet interspersed with hearts in Linda Guffey's celebration of sisterhood. And more!

Heart motifs abound, especially little ones. But there are larger hearts in the samplers from Amy Ambabo-Miller and Tori Mason. Still bigger ones show up in Janet Newland's sampler and in Cynthia Cook's. Hearts combine with other motifs, such as the apples in Carol LaMar's work, and the houses and flowers in Shanon Allen's prizewinner.

There are countless other decorations or ornaments: Karen Montgomery's little landscape, the dogs in Barbara Hill's snow scene, the trees in Linda Pietz's design, Christmas symbols from Rose Saladis, the graceful bow from Amy Ambabo-Miller, the rings in Marylynn Cormier's design.

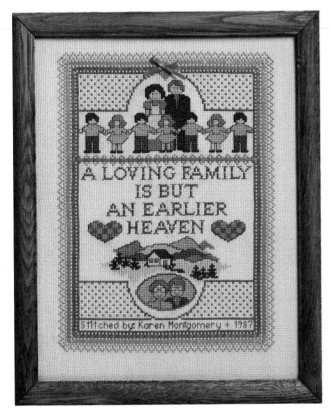

Notice how many of our prizewinning designers combined cross-stitch with *other embroidery stitches.* Laura Jourdan and Janet Newland used French knots to achieve effective three-dimensional effects. Kerry Higginbotham added dimension with Smyrna stitch and Lorraine Wixom's single-strand embroidery created a sampler of great delicacy.

Some of our winners, like Deborah Franks, used *beads* to enhance their designs, and many employed cross-stitch to couch *ribbon* onto a design, as in the work by Dixie Falls and Karen Montgomery.

There is only one first-prize sampler for which we do not give instructions in this volume: *I Pledge Allegiance,* which claimed a first prize for Jane Ballard of Joplin, Missouri. It is extraordinarily demanding, done on very fine linen with fine modeling of the elements in the landscape. But it is also inspiring, so we show it here. Jane is not the only winner to have used metallic thread, but notice how she has employed it to give a realistic sparkle to even the tiniest windows in her picture.

Another interesting aspect of Jane Ballard's work is her departure from the rather standard practice of letting the fabric canvas serve as background. In this, she is like Barbara Hill (*Snowflakes and Children*), whose hanging resembles needlepoint. Do you see any designs in the book that you would like to translate to needlepoint? Many are adaptable.

If you are a cross-stitch addict, you will want to use many of the decorative touches on gifts—pillows, table linens, even collars and cuffs. Use standard fabrics woven especially for cross-stitch, or adapt a border or motif on checked, plaid or striped material, giving you the guidelines needed for precise stitchery.

While you're about it, also shop this book for thoughts on *colored cross-stitch linens.* Our samples of effective color use include the green "slate" on page 119, the small blue hanging on page 105, and the "homespun" backgrounds used for samplers on pages 39, 61, 99, 123, and 199. New colored linens range from white and pastels to dark colors—even black.

Finally, this is a good sourcebook for *matting and framing ideas.* Most of our contestants used professional framing, some with mats to match or coordinate with their embroidery colors. Note the double mat on page 187, for example, and the use of padding to give dimension to the embroideries on pages 23, 109, 128, and 155.

Many contest entries were framed with glass. This is good protection for embroidery, but some specialists in this field prefer to present their work without glass, using a soil-resistant spray to protect the samplers and carefully hand-vacuuming them from time to time.

Framing needlework is a skill to which you may have ideas and expertise to contribute, but which benefits from a professional hand.

Plan ahead for framing by leaving enough border material all around to take care of the frame dimensions. Whoever does the framing will stretch the piece around heavy cardboard or foam core, then staple it on

I pledge allegiance to the Flag of the United States of America and to the Republic for which it stands, one Nation under God, indivisible, with Liberty and Justice for all.

I PLEDGE ALLEGIANCE, a first-prize winner by Jane Ballard of Joplin, Missouri. This designer uses threads like paints. "I just put needle to fabric," she says. "I never make preliminary drawings." She also uses her fabric like an artist's canvas, covering the entire picture area with embroidery. The sampler is very finely worked. French knots create the stars, while the stripes in the flag are stitched 24-to-the-inch, with darker reds in the shadows to give them greater depth. The detail in the village scene is extraordinary, down to the doorknobs and the gilt touches that make the windows sparkle. Jane says she's "very much an amateur"—this is only her third original design. It is such a complex and demanding work, however, that we omit instructions for it in this book.

back. (Beware of anyone who tries to secure the work with cellophane tape, since this can discolor the fabric.)

If you have never designed anything before, notice how many of these prizewinners are the embroiderers' first attempts at design. Cross-stitch is an ideal medium for any designer, amateur or professional. The even weave of the background fabric acts as a perfect guide for stitching. The cross-stitch is also one of the most relaxing stitches to execute, and produces results faster than needlepoint. After all, the closely woven linen used for cross-stitch is meant to show, and there is no need to fill it solidly with stitches.

Needlework can be infinitely satisfying however you pursue it, whether you like to execute another's design, taking pleasure in precise reproduction, or love to experiment, injecting at least one idea that is just your very own in every piece of stitchery.

Expressions of Love

This gallery of samplers documents the lives and feelings of the winning designers. Join them in commemorating an event, honoring an achievement, celebrating an occasion, paying tribute to a relationship, or sharing a favorite saying through the art of counted cross-stitch.

We Love Our Country Home

A second-prize winner by Vickie Alexander
of Seattle, Washington

Here is a celebration of country life that's not difficult for a
newcomer to cross-stitch. The pleasing composition, held in
by running stitches, makes use of the backstitch—sometimes
in contrasting colors—to define many of the homey objects.

About Vickie Alexander

Vickie Alexander and her family have always been on the
move. Her husband's career as a field engineer has taken the
Alexanders from St. Louis, where a neighbor's country decor
inspired her sampler; to Dallas, where she designed and
stitched the sampler; to Chatsworth, California; and
Pascagoula, Mississippi; then north and east to the coast of
Maine.

Vickie's sampler pictures items from the home of her St.
Louis friend, to whom she has given the prizewinning piece
as a gift. This is the first cross-stitch project Vickie has
designed, although she had two years of needlework
experience when she undertook it. Cross-stitching seems to
appeal to all the Alexanders: Vickie's two sons and her
husband also have stitched their own designs.

STITCH/COLOR KEYS

Cross-stitch

Two strands	DMC	Bates
⊟ Pink	963	49
▲ Red	498	20
ⱴ Dusty rose	316	895
⊟ Dusty rose—dark	315	896
⅃ Slate gray	931	921
⟍ Gray—light	415	398
⊠ Gray	414	400
⊞ Green-gray	926	779
ᴳ Blue—light	932	920
⌐ Olive—bright	470	267
⒮ Green	3345	268
⊡ Yellow—pale	746	386
⊤ Gold	676	891
ⱴ Tan	842	376
⊘ Brown—light	841	378
⊙ Cocoa	840	379
◤ Chocolate	839	380
⊙ Brick	355	5968
■ Black	310	403
⊓ White		

----- **Running stitch** (two strands): Slate gray

——— **Backstitch** (two strands)

Lines A:	Gray	F:	Black
B:	Chocolate	G:	Light blue
C:	Cocoa	H:	Light gray
D:	Dark dusty rose	I:	Brick
E:	Green-gray	J:	Red

Use matching colors on all remaining outlines.

PROCEDURE

Read General Directions, pages 205 to 214.

Work cross-stitches where indicated, then work remaining stitches.

Families Forever

By Shanon Finnegan Allen of Sandy, Utah

The hearts and flowers and Wedgwood-blue houses give this delightful accent piece the look of delicate china. Even the fabric, a cream Aida cloth that comes with the fleur-de-lis border printed on it, enhances this soft, genteel feeling.

About Shanon Finnegan Allen

Shanon Allen met her husband, Bruce, when she moved from California to Utah. Shanon and Bruce and their three sons, Britt, Todd, and Brice, all enjoy cross-stitch.

Shanon chose the "Families Forever—Eternal Happiness" theme because it is so strongly stressed in her Mormon faith. This sampler is by no means her first design. She has been cross-stitching for three years, and has designed twenty other patterns, together called Patricia Ann Designs. Shanon's winning sampler joins her other original creations at the Mormon Handicraft display in Salt Lake City, Utah.

SIZE

Finished design area is 7¼" square (inside printed border)

MATERIALS

14-count cream Aida cloth, cut 14" square (*Note:* Fabric with printed border, as shown here, can be purchased in needlework shops or mail-ordered from Mormon Handicraft, 105 N. Main Street, Salt Lake City, Utah 84125; phone 801-355-2141; $4.60 postpaid.)

1 skein embroidery floss of each color listed

STITCH/COLOR KEYS

Cross-stitch

Two strands	DMC	Bates
☑ Blue-gray—light	932	920
☒ Blue-gray	931	921
⊡ Rose—light	778	968
⊙ Rose	223	894
◖ Soft green	502	876

_ _ _ _ _ **Running stitch** (two strands): Blue-gray

PROCEDURE

Read General Directions, pages 205 to 214.

Work cross-stitches where indicated, then work remaining stitches.

Over the Miles That Keep Us Apart

By Amy Ambabo-Miller of Rapid City, South Dakota

This friendship sampler achieves real impact because the stitches are so small and tight that the design fairly bounces off the 22-count Aida cloth. While the exquisite pinks and the light blues are soft, the navy-and-white checkered border and the strong red outline around the border and the intertwined hearts demand attention. Amy heightened the three-dimensional effect by stretching the Aida cloth over a slightly padded mat.

About Amy Ambabo-Miller

The Ambabo-Millers are an Air Force family, and the theme of Amy's sampler reflects the many moves that she, her husband, Lloyd, and their two children have made. She embarked on her prizewinning sampler in the midst of a move from Anchorage, Alaska, to a new base in Rapid City, South Dakota, planning it as a gift for a very close friend she had just left behind. Her hearts, tied together, and the homes shown far apart, reflect her motto.

Amy Ambabo-Miller grew up in a creative household in which there was always a parent or grandparent working on a project. She followed their example, knitting and sewing and doing many embroidery and needlepoint projects. She always keeps her needlework on a scroll frame attached to a "giraffe" stand so she can stop and stitch any time she has a few minutes. Amy also enjoys making porcelain and rag dolls.

ABCDEFGHIJKLMNOPQ
RSTUVWXYZ

1 2 3 4 5 6 7 8 9 10

Over the miles that keep us
apart,
Friendship endures;
Love ties our hearts.

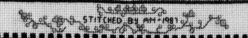

STITCHED BY AM·1981

SIZE
Finished design area is 8⅜″ × 10¾″

MATERIALS
22-count Aida cloth, cut 15″ × 18″
1 skein embroidery floss of each color listed

STITCH/COLOR KEYS

Cross-stitch

	Two strands	DMC	Bates
⒢	Rose	962	76
ⓞ	Pink	776	24
⚋	Pink—dark	892	28
⛶	Cranberry	600	59
⚊	Salmon	760	9
⚫	Peach—pale	948	778
☑	Sky blue	519	167
⟋	Cornflower blue	793	121
⊠	Cornflower blue—dark	792	940
▲	Navy	820	134
⊞	Chartreuse	907	255
	Leaf green	905	258 (backstitch only)
	Leaf green—dark	904	258 (backstitch only)

———— **Backstitch** (one strand)
   Stems and around leaves: Leaf green
   Hearts and flowers, details: Cranberry
   Bow, details on alphabet and numbers: Dark cornflower blue
   Initials and date (substitute your own): Dark leaf green

PROCEDURE
Read General Directions, pages 205 to 214.
   Work cross-stitches where indicated, then work remaining stitches.

To My Parents

By Evonne LaRue Cano of Sanger, Texas

This intricate valentine of a sampler achieves its strong but lacy look by the artistic use of backstitch touches on cross-stitch design elements. Notice how the designer uses both stitches on her elegant alphabet and on the flourishes over the basket. Her striking stylized flowers are all fully outlined in backstitch, as are the scalloped edges. The mat, cut at the corners to echo the outline of the needlework, gives an attractive, finished look to the piece.

About Evonne LaRue Cano

From childhood, Evonne Cano and her sister had tried many kinds of needlework, always with their parents' encouragement. While visiting a friend, Evonne admired the small "paintings" on the wall and learned they were cross-stitched. She bought two country kits, and quickly found that she loved working them. *To My Parents* is her first original design, created in celebration of her parents' wedding anniversary.

Evonne designed and completed the border and alphabet during two weeks of summer driving. By the time she and her husband returned home, the flower basket and poem ideas were formulated. The flowers have special meaning in Evonne's family. "Every summer my family visited my grandparents at the lake. We always had contests to see who could find the most varieties of wildflowers, and no matter what jar they were tumbled in, they were praised for their 'artistic merit.' " So Evonne's sampler also holds special memories of her grandparents.

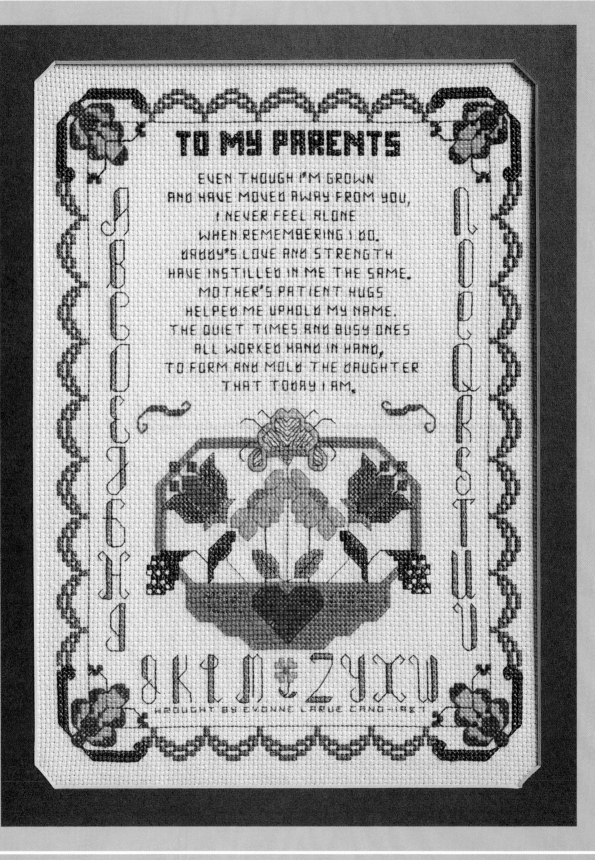

SIZE

Finished design area is 7½″ × 10¼″

MATERIALS

14-count cream Aida cloth, cut 14″ × 17″
1 skein embroidery floss of each color listed

STITCH/COLOR KEYS

Cross-stitch

Two strands	DMC	Bates
☑ Blue	518	168
▲ Slate gray	930	922
◖ Sea green	992	187
⊞ Green—dark	991	189
⊟ Pink—light	818	48
⊙ Dusty rose	3687	69
● Rose—deep	309	42
⋏ Mauve	3042	869
⧄ Peach	754	778
⊠ Brown—light	407	882
Brown	839	380 (backstitch only)
⊡ White		

——— **Backstitch** (one strand)

Note: For clarity, backstitch outlines have been omitted from border scallops and motto title. Outline these areas with matching colors.

  Poem: Slate gray
  Stems (C), veins (D), stamen (E): Dark green
  Stems (F), veins (G): Sea green
  Numbers on basket: Blue
  Names and date (substitute your own): Mauve
  Flowers (A) outline: Deep rose
  Flowers (B) outline: Brown
  Alphabet outline: Dark green
  Use matching colors on all remaining outlines.

PROCEDURE

Read General Directions, pages 205 to 214.

  Work cross-stitches where indicated, then work remaining stitches.

TO MY PARENTS

EVEN THOUGH I'M GROWN
AND HAVE MOVED AWAY FROM YOU,
I NEVER FEEL ALONE
WHEN REMEMBERING I DO.
DADDY'S LOVE AND STRENGTH
HAVE INSTILLED IN ME THE SAME
MOTHER'S PATIENT HUGS
HELPED ME UPHOLD MY NAME.
THE QUIET TIMES AND BUSY ONES
ALL WORKED HAND IN HAND,
TO FORM AND MOLD THE DAUGHTER
THAT TODAY I AM.

WROUGHT BY EVONNE LARUE CANO·19X·

A Baby's Hands Touch So Much . . .

By Kathy Cercone of Milford, Connecticut

This vignette of "life with baby" is presented with an effective frame: the double heart border containing the picture and message. The bold initial letters lend character to the designer's homespun subject.

About Kathy Cercone

Surely no one but a loving mother would design such a happy picture of a naughty child. "I feel the love of your child is a very uncluttered emotion," says Kathy Cercone, who has two youngsters of her own, and works with handicapped children as a physical therapist. Kathy started to design a sampler depicting a handicapped child, then realized that not everyone can appreciate the frustrations of dealing with handicapped youngsters. So she turned to a situation nearly every mother encounters.

It took Kathy six weeks to draw and scale the picture and four weeks to sew it. Kathy's sampler is going to a new niece, her husband's godchild, on her christening.

SIZE
Finished design area is 7″ × 10¼″

MATERIALS
14-count tweed Aida cloth, cut 13″ × 17″
1 skein embroidery floss of each color listed

STITCH/COLOR KEYS

Cross-stitch

Two strands		DMC	Bates
⊞	Gray—light	415	398
☑	Gray	318	399
☒	Blue-gray	932	920
◪	Blue—light	827	159
☑	Turquoise—pale	964	185
☑	Turquoise—light	959	186
◩	Turquoise	958	187
⊡	Pink	605	50
⊚	Rose	3354	74
⊟	Peach	951	366
⊓	Beige	739	885
△	Tan	738	942
▲	Brown	839	380
⊓	Yellow	727	293
■	Black	310	403
⊡	White		
	Golden tan	437	362 (backstitch only)
	Pink—bright	603	76 (backstitch only)
	Blue	826	161 (backstitch only)

——— **Backstitch** (one strand)
Border line (A) and letter on yellow blocks: Golden tan
Pink blocks: Bright pink
Blue blocks: Blue
Baby outline, poem, and initials (substitute your own):
    Brown
Toilet-paper outline: Black

PROCEDURE
Read General Directions, pages 205 to 214.
    Work cross-stitches where indicated, then work remaining stitches.

Yea, I Have Loved Thee

A second-prize winner by Elaine Conetta of Toledo, Ohio

This beauty, with its multicolor alphabet and many borders, displays the greatest variety of stitches of any of the winning samplers: there are twelve different ones used here.

About Elaine Conetta

When Elaine Conetta decided to stitch a sampler to celebrate her wedding anniversary, she charted the alphabet, the border, and the mottoes. That done, she just started stitching and decided on designs and colors as she went along, using scrap material to try out her color and stitch combinations. When it came to the sections solidly filled in with satin and rococo stitches, she skipped charting altogether, picked out colors, began in one corner and kept her fingers crossed that the embroidery would come out even.

Elaine says that with three children at home she did most of her stitching at night, erasing and re-marking the graph-paper squares, longing for a computer to do this for her, and often staying up late to see how sections looked when finished. It took her almost three months to execute the piece, but she managed to finish and frame it just in time for the anniversary.

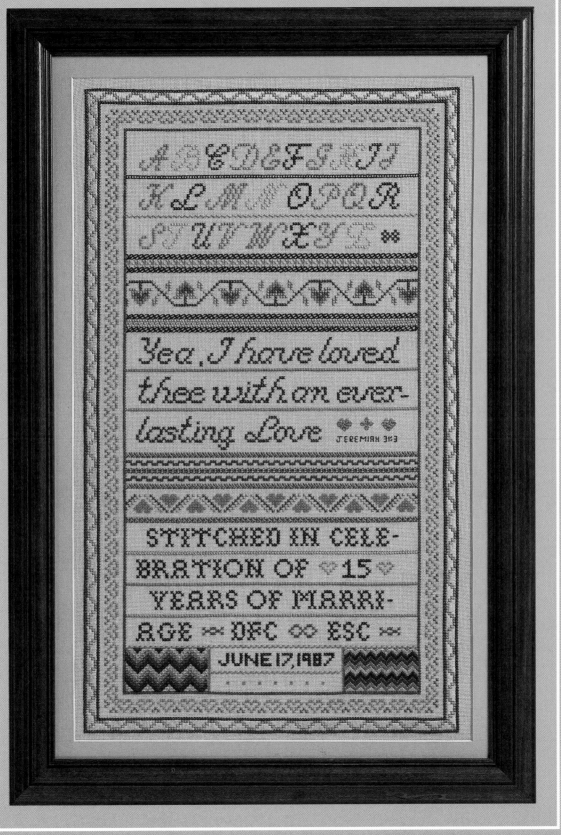

SIZE
Finished design area is 11½″ × 19½″

MATERIALS
25-count natural even-weave linen, cut 18″ × 26″
1 skein embroidery floss of each color listed

STITCH/COLOR KEYS

Cross-stitch

	Two strands	DMC	Bates
▢	Blue—light	3325	159
	Slate gray—light	932	920 (embroidery only)
☒	Slate gray	931	921
	Slate gray—dark	930	922 (embroidery only)
	Gray—pale	928	900 (embroidery only)
⊿	Sea green	368	240
◪	Mint green	563	208
⊞	Forest green	367	216
◉	Green—deep	319	246
⊡	Gold—pale	677	886
	Gold	729	890 (embroidery only)
Ⓝ	Old gold	613	956
⊓	Brick—light	758	868
⊠	Rust	400	351
Ⓢ	Peach	760	9
▽	Rose	3688	66
◖	Rose—dark	3685	70
	Ecru		(satin stitch only)

—————— **Backstitch** (two strands)
"Jeremiah 31:3": Slate gray

PROCEDURE
Read General Directions, pages 205 to 214.

Work all cross-stitches over two threads. Work backstitches. Fill designated areas with embroidery stitches.

Note: Embroidered areas marked with asterisk (*), below, are outlined. Do not work backstitching on these lines; they are guides only.

Work embroidered areas as follows:

A: (on border): Ecru satin stitch all around border
B: Deep-green open chain stitch*
C: Light-blue herringbone stitch*
D: Forest-green star stitches
E: Deep-green plait stitch*

F: Light-brick star stitches
G: Rose Montenegrin cross-stitch*
H: Light-brick plait stitch*
I: Light-blue rococo stitch
J: Four light-blue rococo stitches, rose star stitch in center
K: Plait stitch in two colors (gold in one direction, slate gray in the other direction)*
L: Rust vertical straight stitches
M: Slate-gray star stitches*
N: Work each heart with 20 rose rice stitches*
O: Cross-stitches over cross-stitches (slate gray over gold)*
P: Gold open chain stitch*
Q: Light-brick Montenegrin cross-stitch*
R: Sea-green Montenegrin cross-stitch*
S: Rose herringbone stitch*
T: Rose chain stitch*
U: Fill rectangle with rococo stitches, each zigzag row with a different shade of gray-blue: (1) Dark slate; (2) Pale gray; (3) Light slate; (4) Slate gray
V: Fill rectangle with satin stitch, using same shades of gray-blue as for rectangle U

Using additional letters and numbers, substitute desired date and initials of your own.

Additional Letters and Numbers

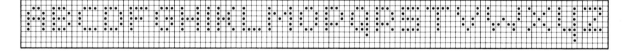

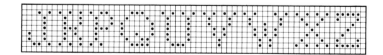

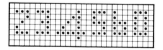

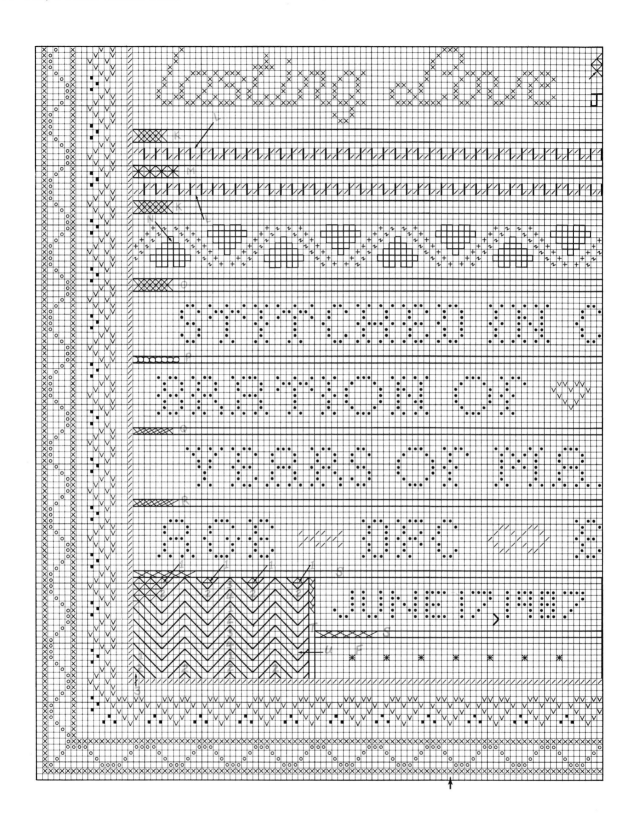

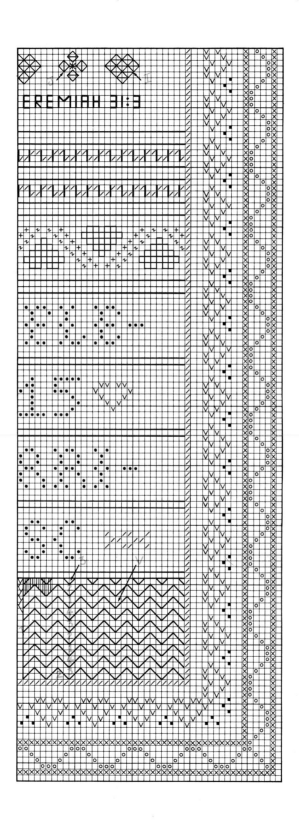

You Have My Heart on a String

By Cynthia Cook of Martinsville, Indiana

This charming sampler took the designer just five hours to stitch; it would be a rewarding project for a beginner. The motto and main subject stand out boldly from the country-brown Aida cloth background. The dramatic effect is carried through in the sampler's open frame, which is formed of hearts and flowers.

About Cynthia Cook

Cynthia Cook's husband inspired her motto: the sampler is an anniversary gift to him. She spent many hours—"and lots of drawing and redrawing"—on the design and then just mixed and matched colors and materials until she found what pleased her, choosing among the Pennsylvania Dutch colors she especially likes. She worked the sampler in the evenings, after her daughters were in bed. For Cynthia, cross-stitch is relaxing.

SIZE
Finished design area is 8³/₄″ × 9″

MATERIALS
14-count Aida cloth, cut 15″ square
2 skeins dark gray embroidery floss
1 skein embroidery floss of other colors listed

STITCH/COLOR KEYS

Cross-stitch

Three strands	DMC	Bates
☑ Red	817	19
◖ Green	3346	257
◎ Purple	553	98
⊡ Peach	353	8
☒ Plum	315	896
◿ Gray—dark	317	400

— **Straight stitch** (two strands): Red

PROCEDURE
Read General Directions, pages 205 to 214.
    Work cross-stitch where indicated, then work remaining stitches.

Marriage Is a Patchwork Quilt

By Marylynn H. Cormier of Orlando, Florida

The frame of traditional quilt patterns is a splendid composition, worked in traditional colors, then accented with gilt running stitches between the words that form the inner border. A bit of gilt thread sparkles in the flower-entwined rings.

About Marylynn H. Cormier

Marylynn Cormier's sampler has a special history: "My husband, Tom, and I had always been close to his brother's four children. When we all lived in New England, it was relatively easy to see them. But in 1979 we and our two (then) toddlers moved to Orlando, Florida. Our nieces and nephews grew up, graduated, and began to marry. Since I felt that we had missed much of their older growing-up years, I wanted to give each one of them a special wedding present—something that would, with care and luck, be passed on to their children. When the eldest married, I designed a patchwork quilt with the building blocks of a good marriage spelled out in cross-stitches. These building blocks (love, patience, commitment, friendship, and so on) now form the inner border of my sampler design.

"When the youngest married, I made a traditional log cabin quilt. On the long ride up to Connecticut, I finally put down on paper the thoughts of marriage that had been churning through my head during the quiltmaking. My motto here is a condensed form of that poem." Marylynn presented the finished sampler to her husband.

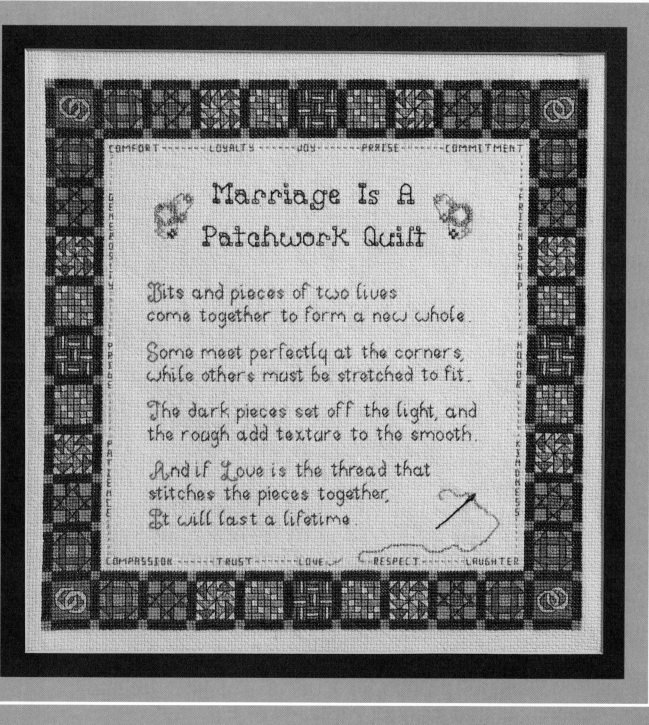

SIZE
Finished design area is 12″ square

MATERIALS
14-count white Aida cloth, cut 18″ square
2 skeins dark blue embroidery floss
1 skein embroidery floss of other colors listed
1 spool DMC gold Fil d'Or Clair (article 282 metallic thread)

STITCH/COLOR KEY

Cross-stitch

Two strands	DMC	Bates
☐ Blue—light	809	130
◪ Blue	799	130
☒ Blue—dark	797	132
⊡ Yellow—pale	3078	292
⊟ Yellow	445	288
◉ Orange—light	743	297
↺ Pink—dark	335	42
☑ Dusty rose	3354	74
◲ Green—light	563	208
◪ Emerald	943	188
▼ Metallic thread		
Gray—dark	413	401 (backstitch and straight stitch only)

_____ **Backstitch** (two strands for lettering, one strand for all other)
     Details in quilt blocks: Dark gray
     Title: Dark blue
     Poem: Emerald
     Capital letters (A): Dark pink
     Border words: Blue
     Vines (B): Emerald
     Thread (D): Metallic thread

_ _ _ _ _ **Running stitch** (two strands) (C): Metallic thread

     Embroider needle (E) with long straight stitches, using dark gray.

PROCEDURE
Read General Directions, pages 205 to 214.
    Work Chart 1. Matching center arrows, work border sections across top of Chart 1, leaving 2 squares of Aida cloth free between inner border on Chart 1 and outer border. Repeat border around Chart 1.

CHART 1

CHART 1

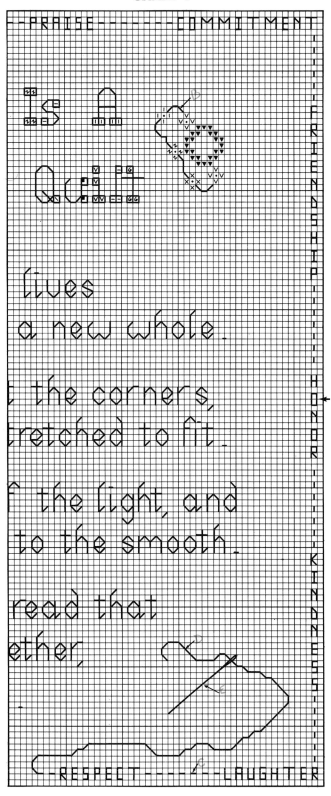

BORDER—LEFT SIDE

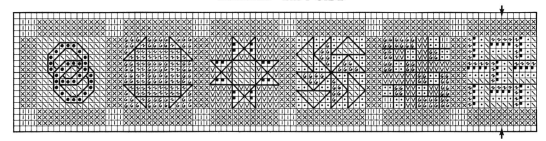

BORDER—RIGHT SIDE

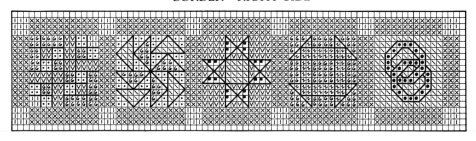

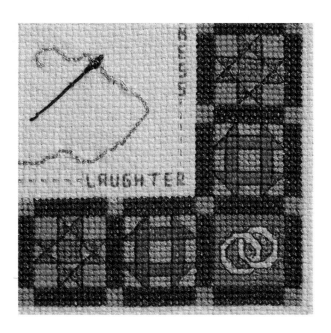

A Mother's Love Is Forever

By Nancy W. Eckert of Mosinee, Wisconsin

A mother and baby caught in mutual adoration express the designer's theme with whimsical charm. Both cross-stitch and backstitch are used, and some of the smooth edges are achieved with partial crosses. The designer flouted the rule that says all the crosses should go in one direction: higgledy-piggledy stitches add texture and an appropriate naive touch to this picture.

About Nancy Eckert

Needlework, Nancy Eckert finds, is an easy way to make new friends. Her husband John's career has taken the Eckerts to four different states in the last eight years. The first thing Nancy does in a new community is to head for the nearest craft shop.

Nancy's daughters, ages 4 and 7, inspired her design. "Dinosaurs were the rage," she says, "and it seemed as if all their clothes were shades of pink or purple." As for the motto, she knew it was right the minute she came upon it, "because I still cherish the love and support I get from my own mom, and I want my daughters to know I will always be there for them."

Nancy spent many hours with graph paper working out her design, she says, but she found the stitching itself easy. John is teaching Nancy how to plan out future projects on a personal computer.

SIZE
Finished design area is 4¾″ × 6¾″

MATERIALS
14-count white Aida cloth, cut 11″ × 13″
1 skein embroidery floss of each color listed

STITCH/COLOR KEYS

Cross-stitch

Two strands	DMC	Bates
☑ Lavender	553	98
▲ Purple—deep	550	102
☑ Turquoise	959	186
☒ Turquoise—deep	958	187
☑ Pink—bright	603	76
☐ Peach	3708	26
⊡ Yellow—bright	973	290
⊞ Orange	970	316
◎ Sand	945	347
◼ Brown—dark	3371	382

———— **Backstitch** (two strands for lettering, one strand for all others)
　　　Flower stem (A): Deep turquoise
　　　All other outlines: Dark brown

PROCEDURE
Read General Directions, pages 205 to 214.
　Work cross-stitches where indicated, then work remaining stitches.

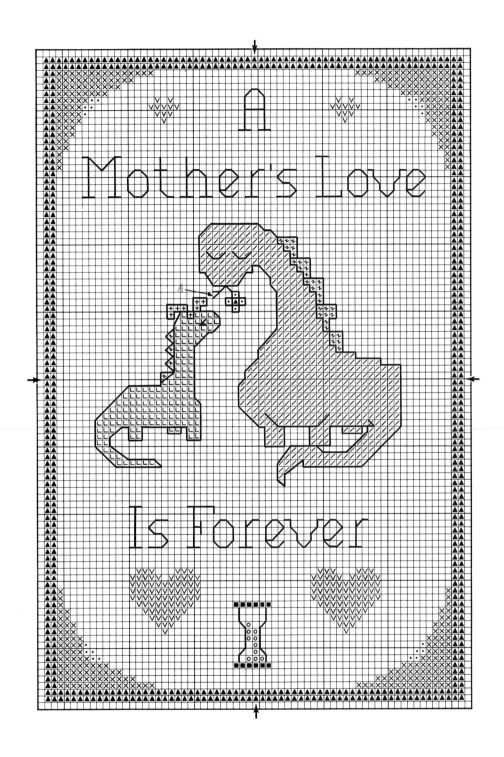

I Love to Knit

Grand-prize winner by Dixie L. Falls of Turner, Oregon

The work of an accomplished needlewoman, this design on natural linen is an amazing montage of knitting tools and the work they produce. It is a masterly mingling of stitches, too. The sweaters, mittens, hand and gloves surrounding the central panel are in needlepoint, worked over one thread. The fisherman's sweater is embellished with chain stitch, fly stitch and French knots. The Tyrolean sweater is lovingly reproduced, complete with bead buttons and free-flowing ties. The center of the innermost border is $\frac{1}{16}''$ narrow ribbon couched with metallic thread. The rest of the sampler is cross-stitched over two threads. All the lettering is in backstitch.

About Dixie L. Falls

Dixie Falls sees needlework as her "life's work." She designs and teaches needlework full time, and her hobbies, making and clothing composition dolls and collecting antiques, are kindred activities. She has won innumerable awards for her knitting and embroidery, and she frequently serves as a judge at needlework competitions. Dixie organized the needlework demonstration at the 1987 Oregon State Fair and used this prizewinning piece to demonstrate techniques. She also takes it with her to Knitting Guild of America conventions.

Dixie is a self-taught needlewoman. Three generations of women in her family were talented at the sewing machine and with paints, upholstering and so on, but did little if any needlework. When she was 4 years old, her mother sat Dixie down in her wicker rocker, handed her a hairnet and two toothpicks, and told her to knit—just so she wouldn't

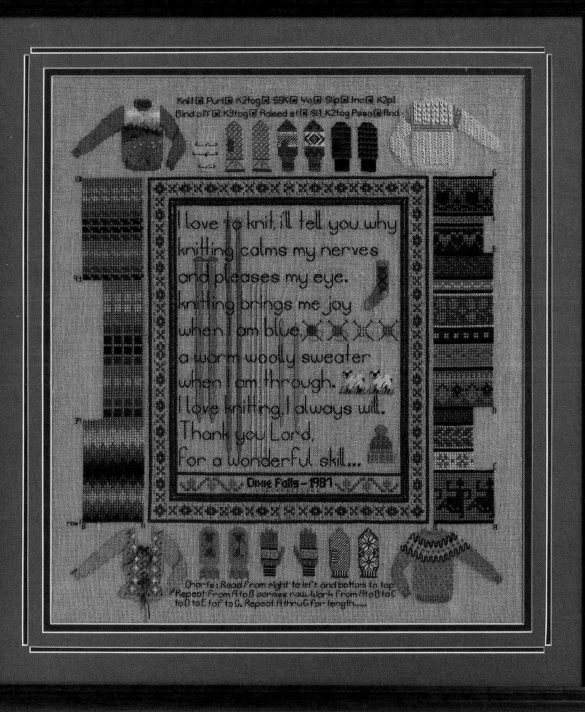

dismantle the sewing machine while her mother was using it. Dixie began working needlework designs when she was 6. This grand-prize sampler is the third of a series of samplers about needlework that she is designing as heirlooms for her children and grandchildren.

Should you ever pass a car with a license-plate holder that says, "She Who Dies with the Most Yarn Wins," that will be Dixie Falls, heading home to be with her husband or with her son James, or off for a visit with granddaughter Jessica and her parents or with grandson Jonathan and his parents, or bound for another needlecraft workshop or event.

SIZE
Finished design area is 13″ × 15½″

MATERIALS
26-count natural even-weave linen, 20″ × 23″
2 skeins embroidery floss each, dark-olive and black
1 skein embroidery floss of other colors listed
1 spool each, No. 5 ecru pearl cotton, DMC gold Fil d'Or Mi-fin
  (article 280 metallic thread), and pearl Balger (glitter filament)
1 yard ¹⁄₁₆″-wide royal-blue satin ribbon
14 green glass seed beads

STITCH/COLOR KEY A FOR CHARTS 1, 4, and 5

Half cross-stitch

	Three strands	DMC	Bates
⊤	Beige	3033	388
▽	Tan	3032	903
▲	Brown	300	352
▼	Brown—dark	3371	382
◣	Rust	356	5975
⊟	Gray-green—light	928	900
◥	Gray-green	926	779
⊠	Gray—pale	3072	397
◩	Gray	318	399
◰	Gray—dark	413	401
⊓	Taupe—light	452	399
⊿	Taupe	3022	8581
⋁	Olive—pale	523	859
⊞	Olive—light	522	859
◤	Olive—dark	520	862
△	Green—bright	905	258
Z	Moss green	3052	859
◿	Soft green	320	216
⊟	Blue—light	828	158
◣	Ocean blue	517	169
◼	Royal blue	792	940
◔	Navy	939	127
⊘	Turquoise—light	807	168
⊔	Turquoise	806	169
◎	Lavender—light	3042	869
Y	Mauve	3041	871
P	Plum	327	101
⊔	Rose—pale	225	892
◥	Peach—pale	950	4146
◤	Burnt orange	976	308
S	Antique gold	3012	844
⊡	Yellow	745	300
◑	Pink—deep	892	28
⊓	Red	817	19
⊠	Raspberry	3607	87
●	Maroon	902	72
◼	Black	310	403
⊡	White		
	Ecru		

_____ **Backstitch**

Read Procedure section, page 64, and see individual instructions for each chart.

PROCEDURE

Read General Directions, pages 205 to 214.

Note: On charts 1, 4, and 5, each square equals 1 *half cross-stitch* over one thread of linen (see exception for Chart 1). On charts 2, 3, and border, each square equals 1 *cross-stitch* worked over two linen threads.

Work Chart 1 first. Matching arrows, work border at lower left corner, then continue border around chart. Leaving a four-thread space, work charts 2 and 3 along side of border. Leaving a four-thread space, work charts 4 and 5 at top and bottom.

CHART 1: Work in half cross-stitch (exception: work four yarn balls in cross-stitch over two threads, following Color Key B).

Loop A: Half cross-stitch with two strands pale gray, one strand glitter filament.

Backstitch (two strands)
Poem: Black
Needles in yarn balls: Dark gray
Backstitch (one strand)
Ski cap: Gray-green
Strands from yarn balls (B): Use matching colors.
Vertical knitting needles: For clarity, backstitch lines have been omitted on chart. Outline using darker shades of matching colors.

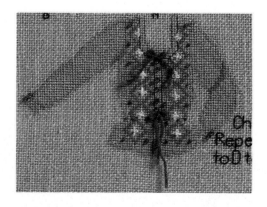

CHART 1

CHART 1

CHART 1

CHART 1

STITCH/COLOR KEY B FOR CHARTS 2 AND 3, BORDER AND YARN BALLS ON CHART 1

Cross-stitch

Three strands	DMC	Bates
▽ Gold	680	901
◨ Antique gold	3012	844
⊡ Yellow	745	300
◪ Burnt orange	976	308
▽ Taupe—pale	3024	900
⊙ Taupe—light	3023	8581
◣ Brown	300	352
■ Brown—dark	3371	382
⊡ Blue—light	828	158
⊟ Air-force blue	932	920
△ Sky blue	322	978
Ⓣ Ocean blue	517	169
◿ Royal blue	792	940
◉ Navy	939	127
◫ Lilac	211	108
◭ Lavender—light	3042	869
⅄ Gray-lavender	341	117
⊞ Mauve	3041	871
⅄ Raspberry	3607	87
◖ Dusty rose—dark	3687	69
▲ Maroon	3685	264
◳ Pea green	472	264
Ⓢ Moss green	3052	859
⊠ Olive—dark	520	862

—————— **Backstitch**

Read Procedure section, page 64, and see individual instructions for each chart.

BORDER: Work in cross-stitch. For lower border, substitute name, initials, or date of your choice in Area A, working half cross-stitch over one thread with dark brown.

Lay ribbon in Area B and couch in place with metallic thread, folding corners neatly.

BORDER

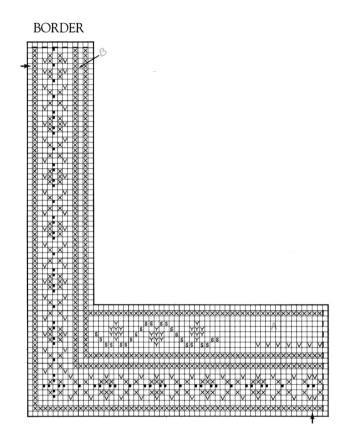

CHARTS 2 AND 3: Work in cross-stitch.
Backstitch (one strand)
Letters and numbers: Black

CHART 2

CHART 3

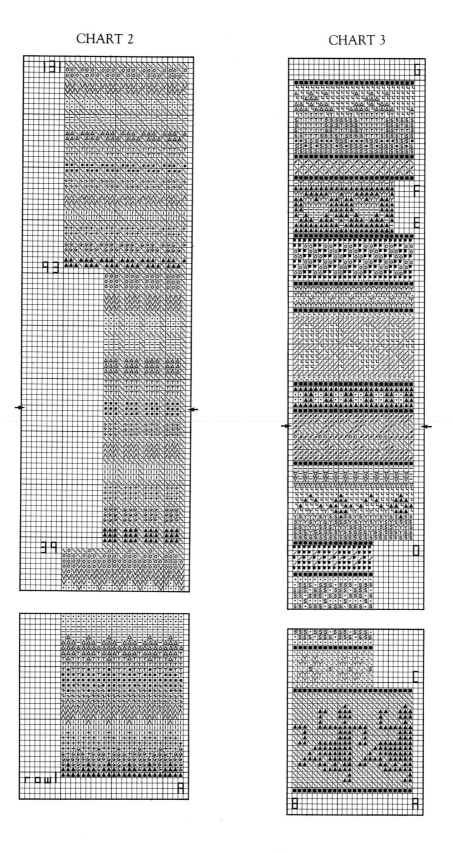

CHART 4: Work in half cross-stitch.
   Backstitch (one strand)
     Hand: Line A: Peach
            Lines B and numbers: Black
            Lettering: Black

Fisherman's sweater (opposite, bottom): Work tan stripes first, then fill sweater with ecru-floss half cross-stitches. Work over these stitches with one strand pearl cotton, using the following embroidery stitches. Do not outline sweater.
   Fly stitch (C)
   Chain stitch (D)
   French knots (E)

CHART 4

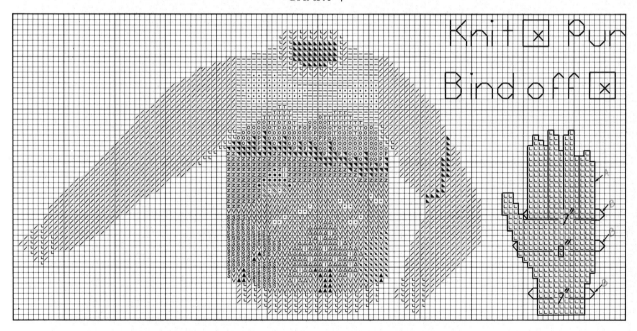

CHART 4

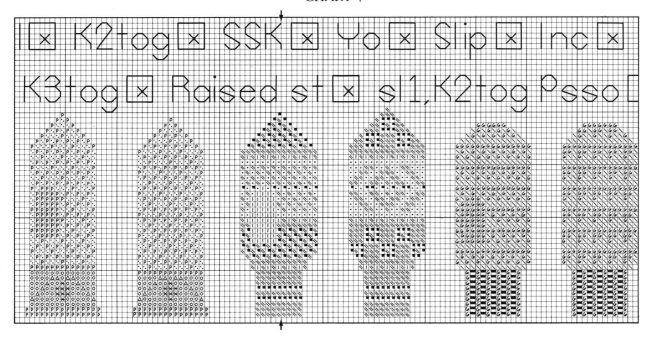

CHART 4

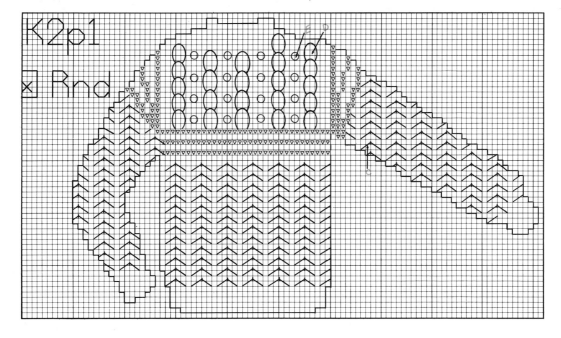

CHART 5: Work in half cross-stitch.
> **Backstitch** (one strand)
> > Left mittens: Lines I: Red
> > > Thumb (J): Black
> > Fingers of gloves: Dark brown
> > Right mittens outline: Royal blue
> > Lettering: Black

Tyrolean sweater (below): Work all half cross-stitches shown, then fill sweater with pale olive.
French knots F: Soft green
Backstitch (H): Soft green
French knots G: Yellow, with white straight stitch
Sew 2 beads to each cuff, 10 beads down front. Tie green-thread bows at neck and waist.

Ski sweater (opposite, bottom): Work all half cross-stitches shown, then fill sweater with lavender. Do not outline sweater.

CHART 5

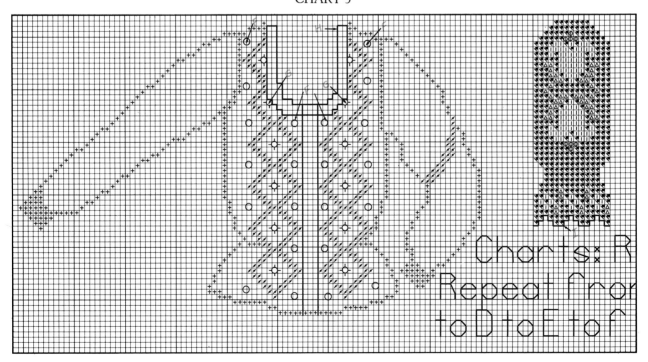

CHART 5

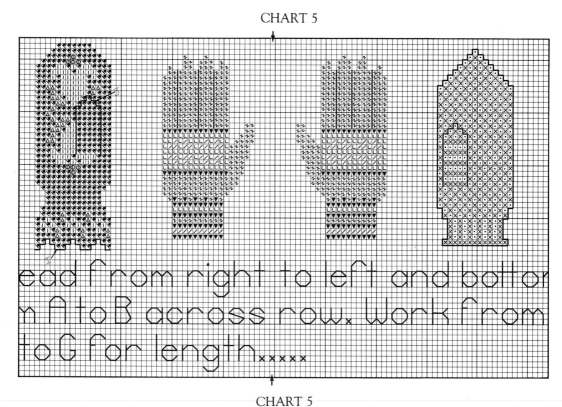

ead from right to left and bottom A to B across row. Work from to G for length.....

CHART 5

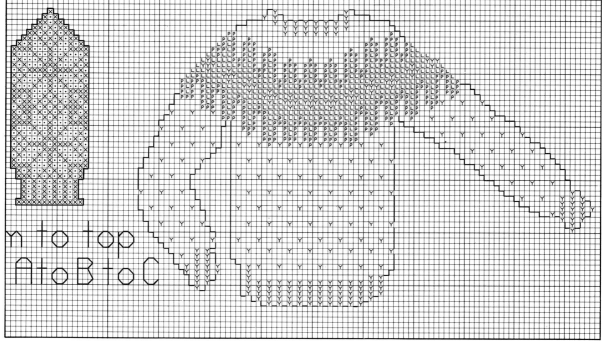

m to top
A to B to C

Love Is the Thread That Keeps Us Together

A second-prize winner by Deborah H. Franks
of Ringwood, New Jersey

The painterly quality of the central figure makes this an outstanding sampler. The little girl, in her blue dress and white pinafore, is rendered with shading that produces a life-like portrait. The overall trellis pattern surrounding the inner flower frame is fashioned with running stitches and held together with seed beads.

About Deborah H. Franks

Deborah Franks says she is a relative novice at cross-stitch, inasmuch as a friend taught her to make simple ornaments only six years ago. She has always been interested in crafts, needlework, and quilting. "At Christmas I've always made my gifts, and even put my work in a consignment craft store." She has also "done lots of holiday boutiques and craft fairs." She chose the sampler motto to describe her life with family and friends: "The bonds that hold relationships together are always love, caring, and sharing."

ABCDEFGHIJKLMN
QPQRSTUVWXYZ
1234567890.

· LOVE ·
IS · THE · THREAD
THAT · KEEPS · US ·
· TOGETHER ·

DHF '87

SIZE
Finished design area is 10½″ × 14″

MATERIALS
14-count tweed Fiddler's cloth or Aida cloth, cut 17″ × 20″
1 skein embroidery floss of each color listed
68 rose glass seed beads

STITCH/COLOR KEYS

Cross-stitch

	Two strands	DMC	Bates
⊡	Rose—light	224	893
☑	Rose	223	894
☒	Rose—deep	221	897
⌐	Soft green—light	503	875
◖	Soft green—dark	501	878
☰	Blue—light	800	128
⊞	Blue	799	130
▲	Royal blue	797	132
Ⅱ	Gray—light	648	900
△	Gray	647	8581
Ⅳ	Gray—dark	645	905
⊠	Cocoa	632	936
Ⓢ	Chocolate	938	381
Ⓝ	Gold—pale	677	886
Ⓨ	Old gold	3045	373
◤	Bronze	831	889
·	Beige	3033	388
Ⓣ	Peach	950	4146
■	Black	310	403

- - - - - **Running stitch** (two strands)
      Trellis lines with beaded flowers: Light rose
      Trellis lines from upper right to lower left: Light soft green
      Remaining trellis lines: Light rose

⊙ **Beads**

PROCEDURE
Read General Directions, pages 205 to 214.

Work all cross-stitches, then running-stitch trellis. Sew beads to trellis flowers, as shown.

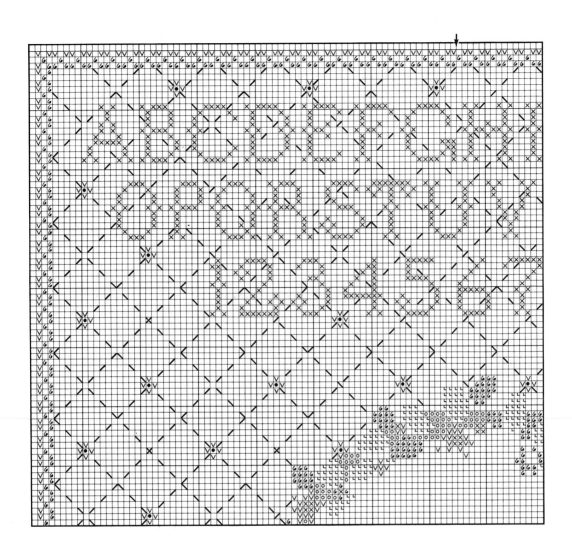

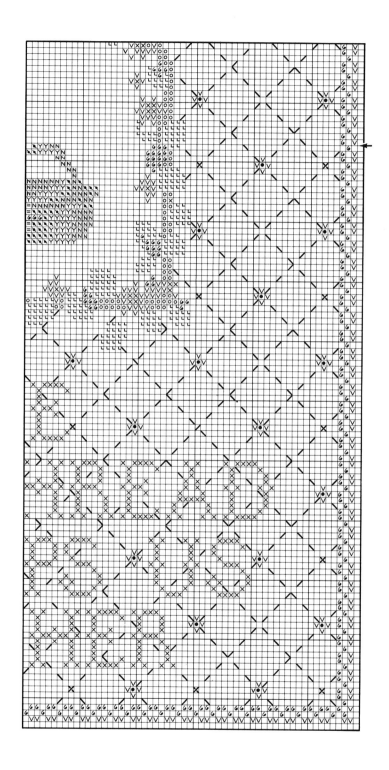

Sisters—So Much Love in One Family

A second-prize winner by Linda T. Guffey
of Riceville, Tennessee

It is the exceptional border design, with alphabets and numbers framing both motto and subject, that won a second prize for this sampler. The design is highly original in its choice of the Kate Greenaway pose for the six sisters, and pleasing in its use of shades of blue, green, old rose, and mauve.

About Linda T. Guffey

The six sisters depicted in Linda Guffey's design are Janie, Suzanne, Linda herself, Martha, Tippy, and Cindy. "We are not only family, but friends. As the middle child in a family of seven (I have an older brother), my life has been truly blessed by being one of six sisters." Hence this tribute, which graces Linda's living room.

Linda credits her mother for teaching that sewing and needlework patterns can be changed in unlimited ways, and says her desire to design surely came about because she had an "annoying habit" of wanting to make changes in graphs. She particularly likes the flexibility of cross-stitch.

As a wife and busy mother of two sons (ages 10 and 7), Linda has discovered that "the most difficult aspect of cross-stitching and designing is finding the time. I'm one of those mothers you see at the pediatrician's office with an embroidery hoop and her latest cross-stitch project."

SIZE
Finished design area is 8″ × 10″

MATERIALS
14-count cream Aida cloth, cut 14″ × 16″
2 skeins embroidery floss each, antique mauve and blue-gray
1 skein embroidery floss of other colors listed

STITCH/COLOR KEYS

Cross-stitch

Two strands	DMC	Bates
⊠ Antique rose—light	224	893
⊞ Antique rose	223	894
◪ Antique rose—dark	315	896
⊘ Antique mauve	316	895
⊡ Soft green	504	213
◖ Soft green—dark	502	876
◹ Peach	951	366
⊓ Teal blue—pale	927	849
⊟ Blue-gray—light	932	920
◉ Blue-gray	931	921
◤ Blue-gray—dark	930	922
Ⓢ Antique violet	3042	869
⬚ Antique violet—dark	3041	871
▼ Gray-black	844	401
⊡ White		

————— **Backstitch** (two strands)
      Lettering: Antique rose
      Lines A: Dark soft green

    Backstitch (one strand)
      Children's outlines: Gray-black

PROCEDURE
Read General Directions, pages 205 to 214.
  Work cross-stitches where indicated, then work remaining stitches.

Like a Quilt, a Family Is at Peace

By Kim R. Hatfield of Savannah, Georgia

This is a wonderfully bright piece, with a very sophisticated, contemporary use of color and design. At first glance, it seems to be simply a roundup of quilt-patch patterns, but look closely: the designer has used only 32 squares (paired to make 16 rectangular units), then lined them up strategically to produce her dazzling central "quilt." Except for the motto, which is backstitched, the piece is worked entirely in cross-stitch.

About Kim R. Hatfield

When Kim Hatfield was a child, she had an old family quilt, and her grandmother entertained her by recounting where each scrap of cloth came from. So it was natural for Kim to select a family quilt theme. It seemed the perfect expression of the way she feels about her family and the relationships they share.

Kim taught herself cross-stitch about three years ago, during her second pregnancy. This prizewinner of hers will hang in her home.

Like a Quilt...
a Family is at peace,
when the pieces are
as One.

SIZE
Finished design area is 10″ × 12″

MATERIALS
14-count cream Aida cloth, cut 16″ × 18″
1 skein embroidery floss of each color listed

STITCH/COLOR KEYS

Cross-stitch

Three strands	DMC	Bates
☑ Pink	761	8
☒ Bright red	606	335
◉ Cranberry	304	47
▲ Maroon	815	43
◥ Purple	327	101
⊡ Yellow—pale	745	300
⊙ Yellow—bright	444	291
☰ Orange	740	316
⊟ Green—pale	369	213
⊞ Green—dark	367	216
⫾ Blue—light	800	128
⚡ Sea blue	799	130
◖ Royal blue	797	132
◪ Taupe	452	10
⊔ Brown—light	436	363
Brown—dark	898	360 (backstitch only)
■ Black	310	403

———— **Backstitch** (three strands): Dark brown

PROCEDURE
Read General Directions, pages 205 to 214.
   Work cross-stitches where indicated, then work remaining stitches.

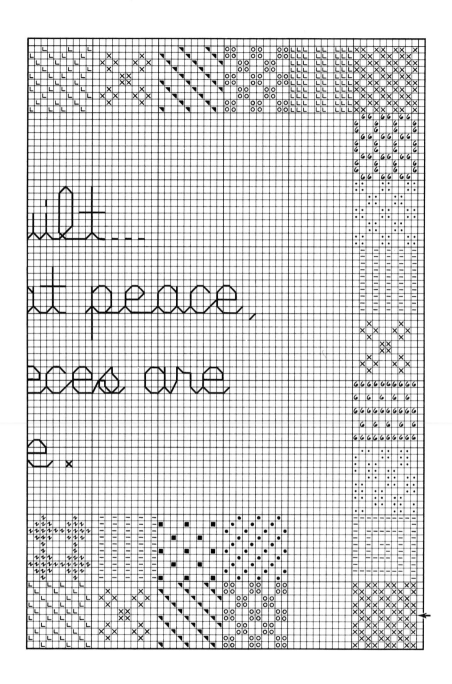

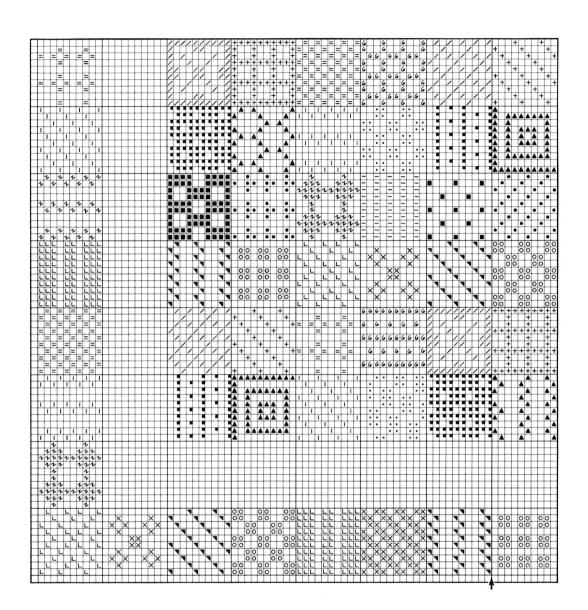

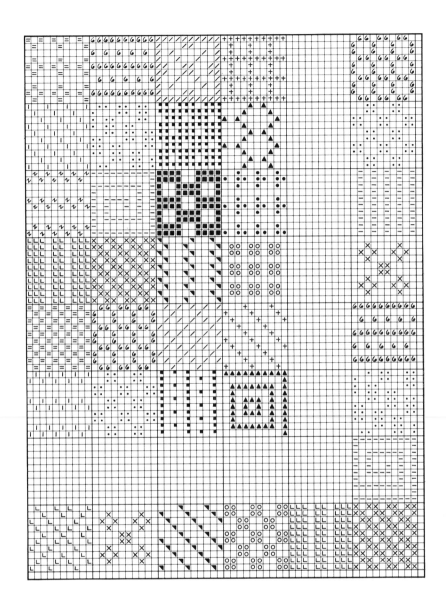

Because of Your Love I Have Blossomed

By Kerry Lea Higginbotham of Russell Springs, Kentucky

This sampler mingles pale blue and peach flowers, then accents them with salmon and touches of tangerine. The whole composition is enlivened by a random sprinkling of salmon crosses on the background. The sampler has more texture than an all–cross-stitch sampler, since the designer departed from cross-stitch in favor of eight-pointed Smyrna stitch in three of her flowers.

About Kerry Lea Higginbotham

When Kerry Higginbotham learned of the "Expressions of Love" contest, she decided to work a contest entry as a gift for her husband. "He was my inspiration," she says. "I know that our love for one another has helped us complement each other, and his love, understanding, and caring have enabled me to grow and be my best. And what better way to show someone's best than to picture flowers blossoming as the result of nurturing and caring for them?"

   Most of Kerry's cross-stitch projects have been small, she says, and she found the sampler a challenge. She estimates that it can be completed in approximately three weeks (maybe four) of leisurely cross-stitching—that is, evenings and one afternoon a week.

SIZE
Finished design area is 7¾″ × 10¾″

MATERIALS
11-count cream Aida cloth, cut 14″ × 17″
1 skein embroidery floss of each color listed

STITCH/COLOR KEYS

Cross-stitch

Two strands	DMC	Bates
⊘ Blue—light	828	158
⊔ Sky blue	813	160
▲ Ocean blue	826	161
· Peach	353	8
⊡ Salmon	352	10
⊠ Tangerine	350	11
◖ Emerald	912	205

———— **Backstitch** (two strands)
Border vine and stems (A): Emerald
Peach border flowers: Tangerine
Blue flowers: Ocean blue
Lettering: Tangerine

✳ **Smyrna cross-stitch** (two strands)
Crosses B: Sky blue
Crosses C: Tangerine

PROCEDURE
Read General Directions, pages 205 to 214.
  Work cross-stitches where indicated, then work remaining stitches.

Children and Snowflakes Are Never the Same

A first-prize winner by Barbara Hill of Hancock, Michigan

Viewed from a distance, this winner could be a painting done in oil. The skiers and their dogs stand out sharply against the thick white snow. The designer abandoned the cross-stitcher's usual reliance on a cloth background and covered her linen fabric entirely with cross-stitch instead. Close up, the sampler has a needlepoint feeling, and the piece would require at least as much time as needlepoint.

About Barbara Hill

Barbara Hill still lives in the town where she was born and raised, in the northernmost part of Michigan as it juts out into Lake Superior. She and her husband, Donald, met on a ski slope, and because they are both skiers, it seemed natural that their boys would ski as well. (The Hills started them on the slopes when they were 2.) Between living in a "winter wonderland" that sometimes gets over 300 inches of snow, and raising Tyler, now 12, and Anders, now 10, Barbara really knows the meaning of her motto.

Barbara began doing needlework at age 8, starting with knitting and soon progressing to crochet, crewel, needlepoint, and, in 1984, her present favorite—counted cross-stitch. This sampler was her fourth to be completed—"One of my other samplers won first prize and Best of Show at our County Fair"—and the first of her own design.

SIZE

Finished design area is 10″ × 16″

MATERIALS

26-count natural even-weave linen, cut 16″ × 22″

3 skeins cream embroidery floss

2 skeins embroidery floss each, light gray, blue-gray, green, garnet, and gold

1 skein embroidery floss of other colors listed

STITCH/COLOR KEYS

Cross-stitch

	Two strands	DMC	Bates
	Blue-gray—pale	928	900
	Gray—light	3024	900
▽	Smoke gray	646	8581
⟋	Garnet	814	44
▲	Forest green—deep	934	862
⟈	Taupe	640	903
∟	Brown	869	944
⊠	Brown—dark	3371	382
⊞	Antique blue	931	921
⊙	Cream	712	387
⊟	Beige	543	933
⊡	Gold	3045	373

———— **Backstitch** (two strands)

Fan window: Forest green

Skis and poles: Dark brown

PROCEDURE

Read General Directions, pages 205 to 214.

Work all cross-stitches over two threads as shown. Fill in background with cross-stitches in colors indicated. Do not work lines A. Using additional letters, substitute names of your choice.

Additional Letters

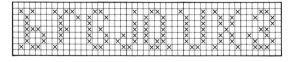

TOP LEFT

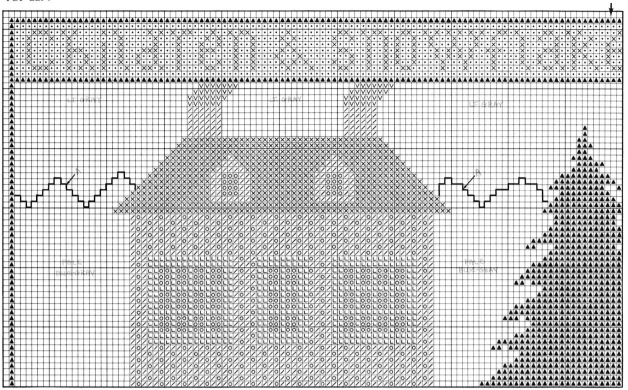

TOP RIGHT

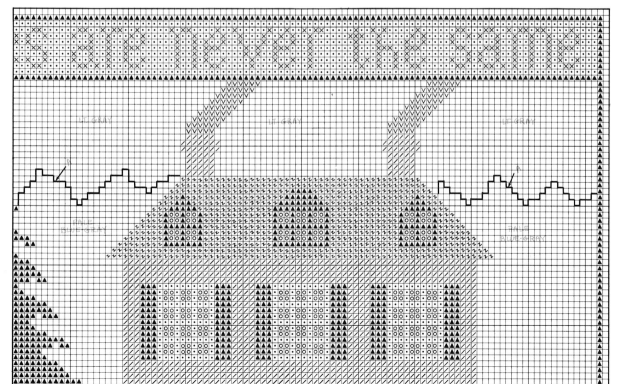

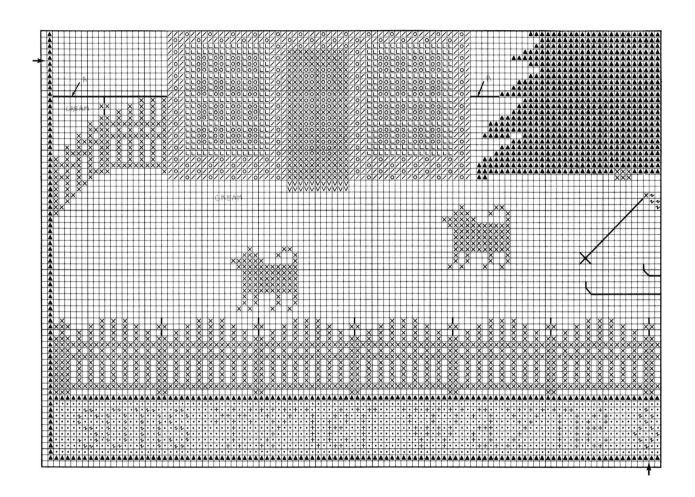

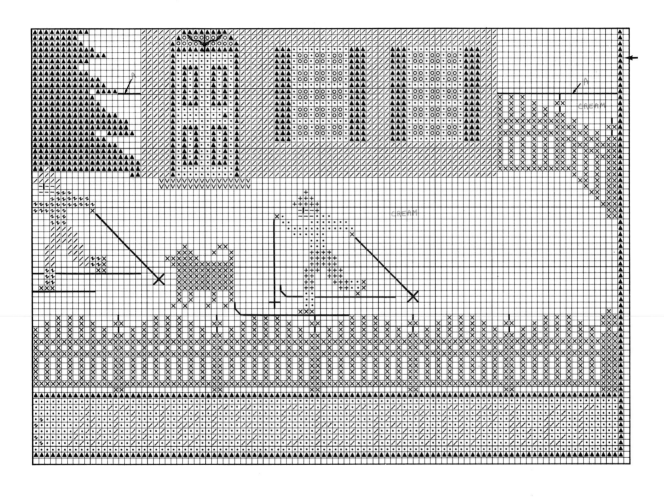

Come, My Dear

By Barbara L. Ihde of Beloit, Wisconsin

In this small hanging the famous Robert Browning sentiment is embellished with a fall of hearts and flowers ending in a lovely lacy heart. It may be stitched on any color Aida cloth and is an ideal first project for a beginner, since it can be completed quickly and easily.

About Barbara L. Ihde

Though Barbara Ihde has done needlework for many years, particularly sewing for herself and her five children, she is relatively new to cross-stitch. Her interest was first piqued by a cross-stitched sampler her niece gave her as a Christmas gift. When her husband retired and they started traveling, she turned to cross-stitch as a diversion—"and soon became an addict."

To celebrate her 35th wedding anniversary in 1987, Barbara chose as her motto a variation on the wish for a long marriage in Robert Browning's *Rabbi ben Ezra.* She will hang the sampler in her bedroom, so she used colors to harmonize with that room's decor.

SIZE
Finished design area is 3″ × 13″

MATERIALS
14-count Colonial blue Aida cloth, cut 9″ × 19″
1 skein embroidery floss of each color listed
6″ × 16″ sturdy backing fabric
2 hangers with slots 4½″ wide

STITCH/COLOR KEYS

Cross-stitch

Two strands	DMC	Bates
▲ Apricot	922	324
☒ Cream	712	387
◖ Green	988	243
Brown	433	371(backstitch only)
Gold	782	308(Smyrna cross-stitch only)

———— **Backstitch** (two strands)
Vertical stem: Green
Poem: Brown

Backstitch (one strand)
Initials (substitute your own): Cream

✳ **Symrna cross-stitch** (two strands): Gold

PROCEDURE
Read General Directions, pages 205 to 214.
Work all cross-stitches and backstitches.
Press sides under, leaving ½″ borders. Fold ends over hangers and sew. Trim lining ½″ larger all around than front; press side edges under ⅝″. Center lining on back, turn top and bottom ends under; pin in place, then blindstitch.

I Believe in Love

By Laura Jourdan of Santee, California

The designer's palette—shades of dusty rose and plum—gives her sampler great character. Some of her other effective design touches are the use of backstitch in the lacy border, the tendrils winding from the top and bottom decorative hearts, and the flower outlines. Laura used the long stitch for the stems and French knots for her Queen Anne's lace. Her finishing does full justice to her lovely needlework: padding under the sampler to plump it up, a matching mat and a bow of narrow ribbons that lends her sampler an eye-catching third dimension.

About Laura Jourdan

"This piece is actually a posthumous tribute to my aunt Kathryn," says Laura Jourdan. "About two years before she died, at age 83, someone asked her what constituted her most important belief. My aunt responded, 'I believe in love.' The colors are my aunt's favorites. I tried to imbue the work with the delicate, feminine feelings she loved and in fact exemplified. In my mind, it will always be 'Aunt Kathryn's sampler.' "

Describing herself as effervescent, redheaded, and compulsive, Laura Jourdan is a single parent with a 21-year-old married daughter and a 20-year-old son in college. She had done needlework for some years ("latch hook, crewel, then on to needlepoint, and for five years exclusively cross-stitch"). This is her first original design, her first stitching contest, and her first win.

SIZE
Finished design area is 8½″ × 11½″

MATERIALS
14-count cream Aida cloth, cut 15″ × 18″
1 skein embroidery floss of each color listed
⅛″-wide satin ribbon, 1 yard each, white, pearl gray, crimson, and burgundy

STITCH/COLOR KEYS

Cross-stitch

Three strands	DMC	Bates
☑ Dusty rose—light	224	893
◰ Dusty rose—dark	315	896
☒ Plum	902	72
△ Peach	754	778
⊡ Ecru		
◹ Beige	543	933
◉ Olive—light	3013	842
◪ Moss green—dark	937	268
◕ Tweed		
Taupe (two strands)	640	903
Brown—light (one	3064	914
strand)	3371	382
Brown—dark		(backstitch only)
White		(French knots only)

──────── **Backstitch** (two strands)
Tendrils on hearts: Moss green
Border: Plum
Poppies (A), stems on Queen Anne's lace (B): Taupe (*Note:* Work stems on Queen Anne's lace with long stitches, broken as shown.)
Lilies (C): Dark brown
Stamen on lilies: Plum

● **French knots** (three strands)
Stamen on lilies: Plum
Queen Anne's lace: White (two strands), taupe (one strand)

PROCEDURE
Read General Directions, pages 205 to 214.
  Work cross-stitches, backstitches, and French knots. Add initials and date in corner, if desired. Hold ribbons together and make bow at center. Tack knot to sampler at D. Trim ends diagonally.

My Life Was in Apple-Pie Order

A second-prize winner by Eunice J. Koch
of Lawrenceville, Georgia

The sentiment may have an old-fashioned ring: All those
hearts and apples, the colors, and especially the checkered
border hark back to fragrant country kitchens. But the bold
treatment of the fruit bowl, the ice-cream maker and the pie,
and the dramatic deep-green mat, make a strong contemporary
statement.

About Eunice J. Koch

Eunice Koch has an interesting story: "I have been divorced
for close to 25 years. I raised three sons, one of them now
married with two children. I have a challenging career
working with computer software, am active in my church,
am an incurable concertgoer, love museums and galleries,
knit and sew in addition to doing cross-stitch, and read lots.
(My house is not the neatest.)

"In other words, I have a very full, interesting life, which
I thought was complete. Then I met a fine Christian
gentleman (equal accents on *Christian*, *gentle*, and *man*). I
chose colors that Gil likes, and am giving the piece to him."

SIZE
Finished design area is 7″ × 11″

MATERIALS
14-count cream Aida cloth, cut 13″ × 17″
1 skein embroidery floss of each color listed

STITCH/COLOR KEY

Cross-stitch

Two strands	DMC	Bates
⬀ Soft green—pale	369	213
⊟ Soft green	368	240
▼ Soft green—dark	320	216
⬚ Green—light	993	186
⊡ Green—dark	991	189
⊠ Pink	335	42
⬦ Rose	3688	66
⊞ Red	321	47
◉ Red—dark	816	44
⬊ Blue—pale	800	128
⬝ Blue—light	799	130
Ⓨ Blue	798	131
◣ Royal blue	797	132
⬑ Cream—pale	746	386
⬝ Cream	677	886
⊤ Beige	738	942
⊟ Tan—pale	739	885
⬚ Brown—light	435	369
◼ Chocolate	3371	382
⊠ Gray—light	415	398
⬗ Gray	414	400
Ⓢ Gold—light	676	891
⊔ Peach—light	754	778
⊞ White		

———— **Backstitch** (two strands)
    Lettering: Chocolate

Backstitch (one strand)
    Motif outlines: Chocolate

PROCEDURE
Read General Directions, pages 205 to 214.
Work cross-stitches where indicated, then work remaining stitches.

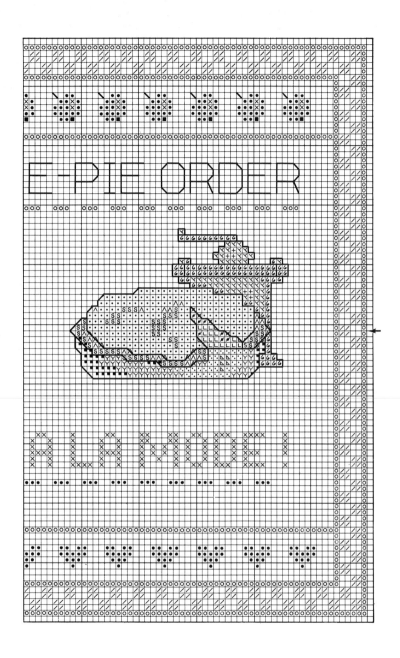

Those Who Love Teaching

A second-prize winner by Carol LaMar
of Guymon, Oklahoma

A strikingly original tribute to a teacher, this sampler could celebrate any student's good experience in school. Look at the paraphernalia all of us remember from the classroom—the Pink Pearl eraser, the No. 2 pencils, the crayons. Carol LaMar chose a green Aida cloth and a plain wood frame to suggest an old-fashioned school slate. We include the alphabet so that you can fill in the name of the teacher you wish to honor.

About Carol LaMar

Carol LaMar had been on vacation, so found out about the contest very close to the deadline. "I designed [the sampler] on Thursday night and Friday, stitched Saturday, Sunday and Monday, framed it Tuesday, photographed it Wednesday and had it in the mail by Friday."

Carol is an experienced needleworker who has been embroidering, knitting, sewing, needlepointing, and quilting for many years. She has been doing cross-stitch for eight years. "I am lucky in having a wonderful husband and two special sons, Matt and Mike, who are tolerant of my sewing."

Carol works as a volunteer teacher's aide in the Transitional First Grade (T–1) at the elementary school in Guymon, Oklahoma. She loves to make things for her church and for the people in her life, and created this sampler for her supervising teacher and friend Mary Ann Earls.

Carol stitches whenever she has a chance. She keeps a small piece in her purse to work on during those "lost minutes"—while waiting at the doctor's office, waiting to pick the kids up from ball practice, or while traveling.

SIZE
Finished design area is 6″ × 7½″

MATERIALS
14-count green Aida cloth, cut 12″ × 14″
1 skein embroidery floss of each color listed

STITCH/COLOR KEYS

Cross-stitch

	Two strands	DMC	Bates
⊡	Aqua—pale	964	185
⊡	Aqua—light	959	186
◣	Aqua	958	187
☑	Pink—light	3354	74
⊞	Pink	962	76
⊙	Red	817	19
◨	Green—pale	564	203
↗	Green—bright	703	238
⊟	Yellow—pale	3078	292
Ⓢ	Yellow	744	301
⊟	Yellow—dark	972	298
Ⅱ	Gold	725	306
⊔	Tan	437	362
⊡	Orange—light	3341	328
◩	Orange	3340	329
⊡	Lavender	340	118
◖	Purple	333	119
◼	Black	310	403
⊠	White		

────── **Backstitch** (two strands)
     Lettering: Black

     Backstitch (one strand)
       Lines A: White
       Motif outlines: Black

PROCEDURE
Read General Directions, pages 205 to 214.
   Work all cross-stitches shown. Using additional letters, substitute names of your choice. Finish with backstitching.

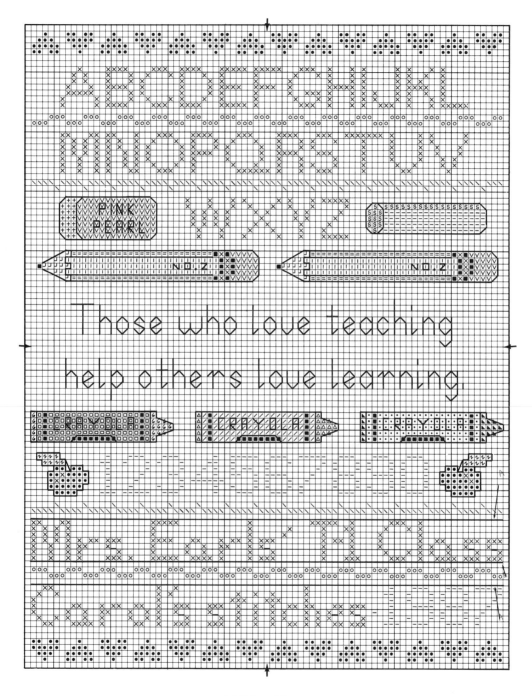

Those who love teaching
help others love learning.

Additional Letters

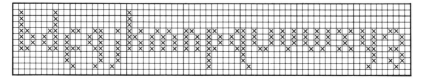

You Are the Golden Thread Connecting the Pieces of My Life

By Denise Longhurst of Mendon, Utah

The homespun motto and its cross-stitched frame are made extraordinary by the designer's surprising and sophisticated color choices. The metallic gold thread used for the motto also outlines all the stars, and the two greens combine with yellow and coral to make a pretty, contemporary palette. The piece is worked on a loose-weave linen, with two strands over each two threads. It would be a good project for a newcomer to counted cross-stitch.

About Denise Longhurst

Denise Longhurst, inspired by a patchwork quilt, uses quilt "pieces" here to symbolize the many facets of her life held together by the golden thread of love she and her husband share. Denise has enjoyed needle arts since her mother first taught her cross-stitch at age 6, and the first sampler she ever completed still hangs in her home today. Her prizewinning sampler complements the decor of her living room, where it will hang.

SIZE
Finished design area is 13¼″ square

MATERIALS
26-count natural even-weave linen, cut 20″ square
2 skeins embroidery floss each, dark moss green, light yellow, and coral
1 skein light moss green embroidery floss
4 spools DMC gold Fil d'Or Clair (article 282 metallic thread)

STITCH/COLOR KEYS
Cross-stitch

Two strands	DMC	Bates
✔ Moss green—light	369	213
● Moss green—dark	367	216
⊡ Yellow—light	745	300
⊿ Coral	352	10
⊠ Metallic thread—gold	282	

PROCEDURE
Read General Directions, pages 205 to 214.

Work all cross-stitches over two threads. Work Chart 1 in center of fabric. Matching inner arrows on border to top and side arrows on Chart 1, work one-quarter border, as shown, at upper right corner of Chart 1. Repeat border at upper left corner, but do not repeat center stitch. Repeat border on lower half of Chart 1 (do not repeat center stitches), and reverse yellow and dark moss green on points of bottom 2 stars (see photograph).

CHART 1

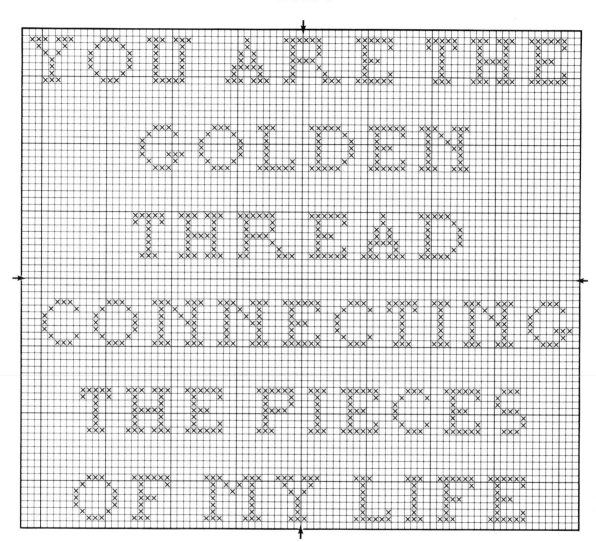

BORDER (ONE-QUARTER)

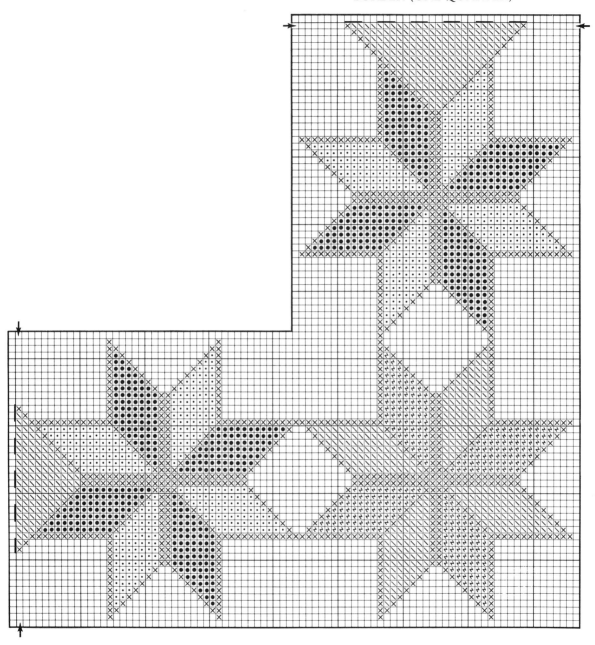

Love for a Grandparent

By Tori G. Mason of Topeka, Kansas

This celebration of the bonds between grandparents and granddaughter relies on hearts, and more of the same, to get across its message. What makes the piece exceptional is the designer's success in achieving a dramatic composition while using subtle, muted shades in the patchwork hearts. Her choice of a stark white Aida cloth sets off her well-weathered colors, as do the sturdy, dark-wood frame and (look closely!) the padding over which she stretched the sampler on its mat.

About Tori G. Mason

Tori Mason works full-time as an animal keeper at the Topeka Zoological Park, where she is in charge of the Tropical Rainforest exhibit. There she cares for birds, also tamarins (small monkeys), iguanas, and crocodiles.

So her love for animals came to mind first when she started thinking about the cross-stitch contest. "However, after sitting and staring for 30 minutes at a blank sheet of paper that said ANIMALS at the top, I decided I needed a new topic. Then I thought about my grandparents, Elvin and Louise Richwine of rural Erie, Kansas, and how much I love them and how close our family is." One hour later, Tori says, she was looking at an almost-finished design, complete with her motto, the patchwork hearts, and the borders.

"But there was a big blank space in the middle. So next day I excitedly took my rough draft to the zoo to show to coworkers. 'It's all finished,' I said, 'but I don't know what to put in the middle.' Cindy Bjork, a large-cat and hoofstock keeper, suggested grandma and grandpa faces." Tori knew that was exactly right.

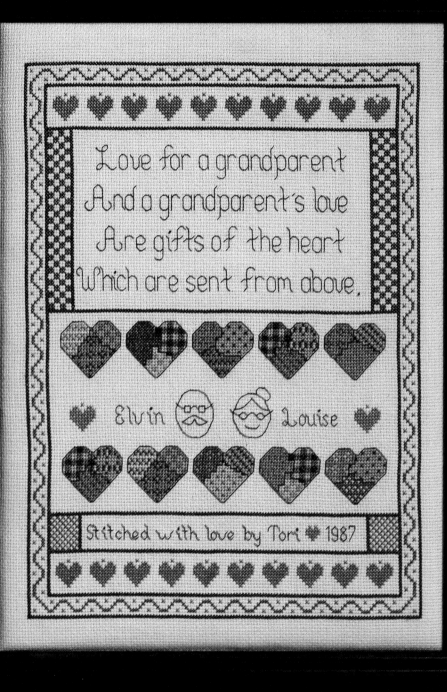

SIZE
Finished design area is 9¾″ × 13″

MATERIALS
14-count white Aida cloth, cut 16″ × 19″
1 skein embroidery floss of each color listed

STITCH/COLOR KEY

Cross-stitch

Two strands	DMC	Bates
⊡ Rose—pale	225	892
🄰 Rose—light	224	893
☑ Rose	223	894
◣ Rose—dark	221	897
△ Antique rose	316	895
◖ Antique rose—dark	315	896
◩ Gray-blue—light	932	920
◪ Gray-blue	931	921
☒ Gray-blue—dark	930	922
Charcoal—dark	413	401 (backstitch only)
⊡ Teal blue—light	598	167
⊡ Teal blue	597	168
⑤ Mauve—light	3042	869
▲ Mauve	3041	891
⊟ Green—pale	504	213
⊞ Green—light	503	875
⊡ Green—dark	501	878

——— **Backstitch** (one strand): Charcoal

PROCEDURE
Read General Directions, pages 205 to 214.

Work all cross-stitches shown. Work backstitches, substituting name and date of your choice.

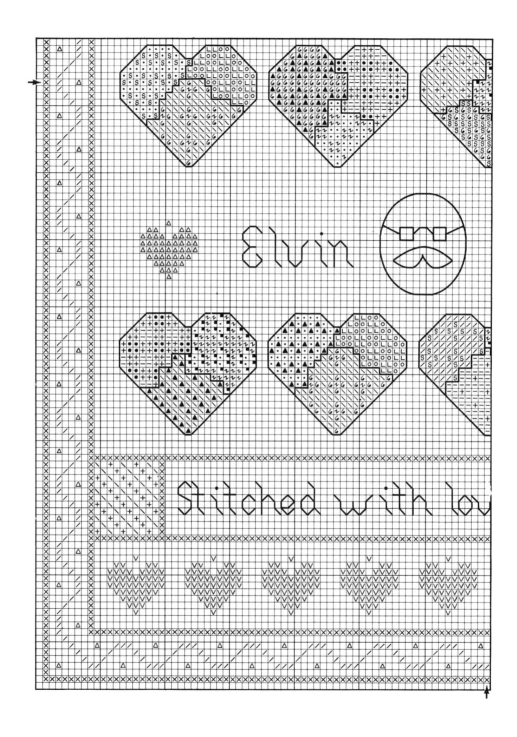

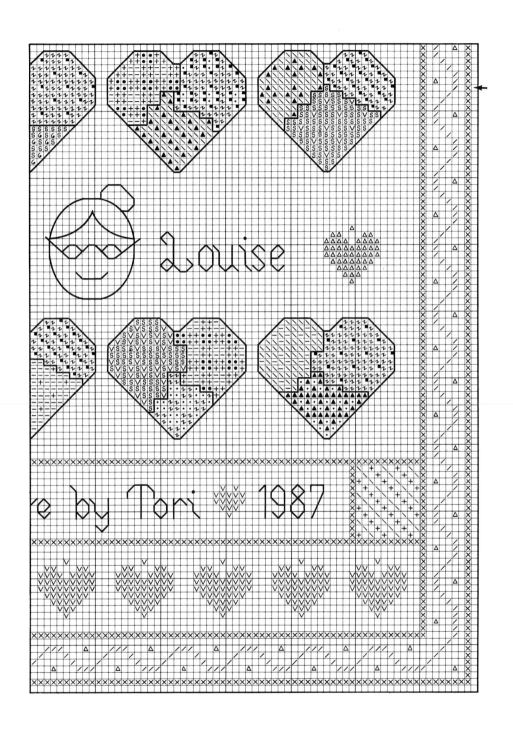

A Loving Family Is But an Earlier Heaven

A second-prize winner by Karen Montgomery of Clearwater, Florida

This lovely three-generation remembrance is a quintessential valentine with a beribboned border. It is done in three shades of peach and features two bands of satin ribbon couched with cross-stitch. There are other delicate touches here: the background of cream Aida cloth, the pink cross-stitches in the blue lettering, the zigzag backstitches (or half cross-stitches) in the mountain behind the house, the vertical backstitches that form the grass. The designer's pale colors work well, since the greens she uses (especially the spruce green in the trees and the father's suit) so successfully define her composition.

About Karen Montgomery

Karen Montgomery describes herself as "a traditional person who chose to stay home after my children were born." She has a degree in interior design. Several of her original designs have been published nationally.

For her contest sampler, Karen used the colors in her home. The ribbon insertion is a technique she developed to trim her daughters' dress yokes. She worked on her sampler for two months—"but I always have several projects going at a time." Karen particularly enjoys cross-stitch because it is so portable. "I stitch while the kids are in the pool, and take projects to the park and even to the dentist's office."

A LOVING FAMILY
IS BUT
AN EARLIER
HEAVEN

Stitched by: Karen Montgomery ★ 1987

SIZE

Finished design area is 8¾″ × 12″

MATERIALS

14-count cream Aida cloth, cut 15″ × 18″
1 skein embroidery floss of each color listed
⅛″-wide double-faced satin ribbon, 1⅝ yards dark peach and 1¼ yards light peach

STITCH/COLOR KEYS

Cross-stitch

Two strands	DMC	Bates
⊟ Gray-blue—pale	928	900
V Gray-blue—light	927	849
☒ Gray-blue	931	921
◪ Gray	318	399
⊡ Peach—pale	948	778
⧄ Peach—light	353	8
↯ Peach—dark	356	5975
⊞ Tan	436	363
● Brown—dark	839	380
O Pink	761	8
☰ Green—light	504	213
6 Green	502	876
▲ Spruce green—dark	501	878
L Yellow—pale	745	300

——— **Backstitch** (one strand)
See below for large crosses.
Mother's and father's mouths: Dark peach
Lines A: Gray-blue
Lines B: Light green
Name (C) (substitute your own): Green
Work all remaining backstitches dark brown

PROCEDURE

Read General Directions, pages 205 to 214.

Work cross-stitches where indicated. Work light green vertical backstitches, then work gray-blue straight stitches on the diagonal.

Large crosses: Pin dark peach ribbon in crosses area below children. Fasten in place with large cross-stitches in light green. Leaving 3″ ends at center top for bow, fasten dark peach ribbon around inner border with dark peach crosses, folding ribbon diagonally to turn corners and working straight stitches over corners as indicated. Tie bow and tack. Fasten light peach ribbon with light peach crosses around outer border.

But Now Abide Faith, Hope, Love

By Janet Newland of Escondido, California

This ambitious sampler has a beautifully worked border design: the motto inspired by 1 Corinthians runs between a cross-stitched frame and a backstitched vine. Other distinguishing touches are the hearts and anchors and the floral tapestry heart, with a scattering of pale-gray French knots to give the heart dimension.

About Janet Newland

Janet Newland grew up in a family that enjoyed needlework. Her paternal grandmother was a quiltmaker, her maternal grandmother was a knitter, and her maternal grandfather used to tat. Her mother was her needlework teacher. Janet's daughter loves counted cross-stitch and needlepoint, too.

This is the second cross-stitch piece Janet has designed. She chose the "Love Chapter" from the Bible because she feels it encompasses all the expressions of love. It was part of her wedding ceremony and has special meaning for her. Janet's design elements have their own symbolism, she says: the flowers symbolize romance, the heart stands for love, and her unbroken vine border says that "life and love are unending." Even her colors are symbolic. Blue is for love, red for passion, and the white background for purity.

Janet works full-time as a church secretary, and has a husband and two children, ages 23 and 19. She had to find minutes during lunch breaks to work on her sampler, and it even went in her backpack when the Newlands took a backpacking trip in Yosemite.

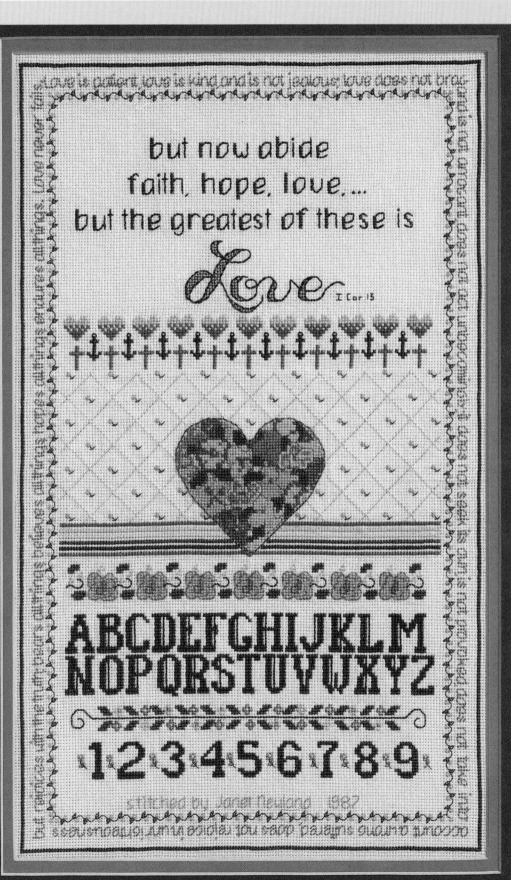

SIZE
Finished design area is 9″ × 14½″

MATERIALS
18-count white Aida cloth, cut 15″ × 21″
2 skeins dark blue-gray embroidery floss
1 skein embroidery floss of other colors listed

STITCH/COLOR KEYS

Cross-stitch

	Two strands	DMC	Bates
⊡	Gray—pale	762	397
☑	Blue-gray	932	920
☒	Blue-gray—dark	930	922
◪	Pink	3689	49
◩	Dusty rose—pale	778	968
◉	Rose—dark	3687	69
◖	Antique rose	223	894
◣	Brown	840	379
◪	Green—dark	501	878
⊟	Mauve—dark	3041	871
⊞	Yellow—pale	677	886

—— **Backstitch** (one strand)
    Vine (A) and stems (B): Dark green
    Outlines within heart: Dark rose

Backstitch (two strands)
    Line C: Dark green
    Border lettering: Blue-gray
    Name and date (substitute your own): Pink
    All other lettering: Dark blue-gray
    Heart outline: Mauve
    Flowers (D): Outlines: Antique rose
               Centers: Dark rose
    Background trellis (E): Pale gray

● **French knots** (two strands)
    Heart (24 French knots scattered around): Pale gray
    Knots (F): Blue-gray

PROCEDURE
Read General Directions, pages 205 to 214.
    Work cross-stitches where indicated, then work remaining stitches.

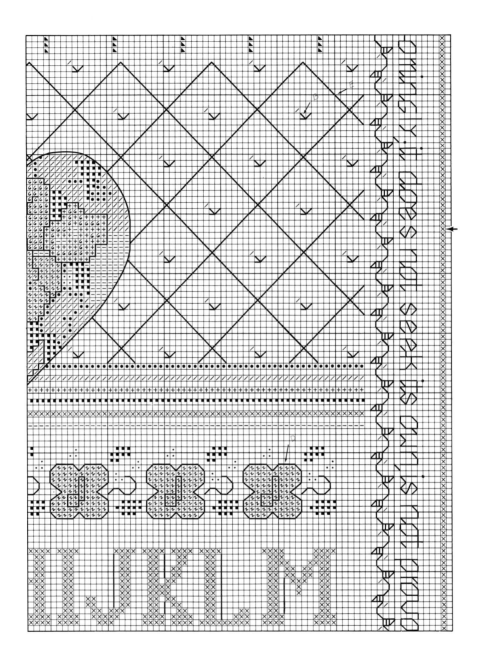

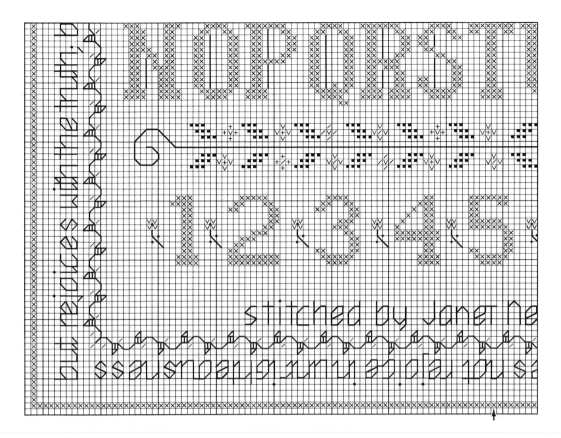

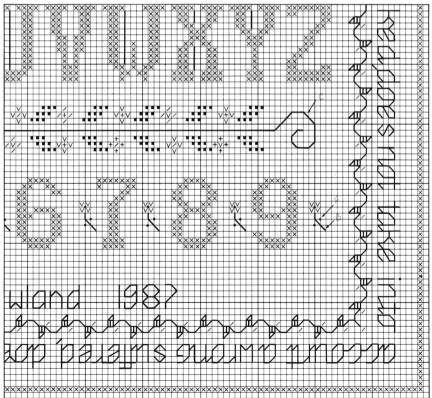

At Eventide the Heart Doth Rest

By Bonnie Patterson of Hamilton Township, New Jersey

This sampler achieves old-style charm with the use of words split to fit the maker's composition and by cross-stitching the twining flowers in a free style suggestive of crewel work. That this is a contemporary piece is clearly announced by the shadow ribbon border and the double mounting with a generous off-white mat.

About Bonnie Patterson

Bonnie Patterson is a self-taught needleworker, and this is her first design project. Cross-stitch is a good medium for a fledgling designer, she thinks, since form and color count more than the use of many different stitches.

Bonnie's love affair with samplers began when she saw a 1832 sampler worked by one of her ancestors. Ever since, she has hunted samplers in antique shops and through publications such as *Early American Life.*

Early samplers were the inspiration for Bonnie's design. They also inspired her motto, though she wrote the verse herself. Her intent was to create a saying that embodied the early settlers' values, "combining love and work, where hands were never idle."

A B C D E F G H I J K L
M N O P Q R S T U V W

a b c d e f g h i j k l m n o p q r
s t u v w x y z 1 2 3 4 5

At eventide the Hea
rt doth rest When lo
ving hands ♥ have
wrought their Best

SIZE
Finished design area is $8^{1}/_{2}'' \times 11^{1}/_{2}''$

MATERIALS
14-count cream Aida cloth, cut $15'' \times 18''$
2 skeins light olive embroidery floss
1 skein embroidery floss of other colors listed

STITCH/COLOR KEYS

Cross-stitch

Two strands	DMC	Bates
⊙ Dusty rose—light	224	893
⦿ Dusty rose	223	894
◖ Rose—deep	3350	42
⊠ Maroon	315	896
⊓ Blue-gray—light	927	849
⊞ Blue-gray	926	779
▲ Gray—dark	413	401
⧄ Olive—light	3013	842
⊻ Olive	3052	859
◼ Green—dark	3362	862
⊡ Gold	676	891
⨪ Tan	3032	903

PROCEDURE
Read General Directions, pages 205 to 214.
  Work cross-stitches where indicated.

Joined in Holy Marriage

By Gail Lea Peters of Vista, California

An utterly charming piece made as a gift, this ringbearer's pillow takes its color scheme from the wedding it commemorates. The pistachio green picks up the color of the matron of honor's and flower girls' dresses, and the peach that of the bridesmaids' gowns. The final touch is achieved by the two golden rings knotted together with ribbons.

About Gail Lea Peters

Gail Peters wanted to make a very special gift—she was thrilled when Celeste and Harold announced their wedding plans and asked her children to be part of the ceremony! Kelly, age 7, was to be a flower girl, and Nicholas, age 5, the ringbearer.

She finally settled on a pillow for the ringbearer to carry, and decided to design it herself when she could find no pattern or kit that fully expressed her feelings.

Gail is a self-taught cross-stitcher. This was only the second project she had ever tackled, and the first she designed. A preschool teacher, she worked the pillow during her summer break. The bride and groom display her gift in an antique showcase.

SIZE
Finished design area is 10″ × 10½″

MATERIALS
14-count cream Aida cloth, cut 14″ × 14″
1 skein embroidery floss of each color listed
14″-square backing fabric
½ yard 45″-wide fabric for ruffle
3½ yards 2½″-wide scalloped lace
12″-square pillow form
¾ yard each pale peach and peach ⅛″-wide double-faced satin ribbon
2 dime-store rings

STITCH/COLOR KEYS

Cross-stitch

Two strands	DMC	Bates
⊡ Peach—pale	353	8
⊠ Peach	352	10
⊙ Pistachio green	369	213
Rose brown	407	882 (backstitch only)

———— **Backstitch** (two strands)
Lettering and rings: Rose brown
Stems on flowers, hearts: Pistachio

PROCEDURE
Read General Directions, pages 205 to 214.

Note: The top and bottom arrows appear to be off-center; when the border is added to left side, the arrows will be centered.

Work all cross-stitches shown. Repeat the border on the left side. Work the backstitch lettering, substituting names and date of your choice.

To make the pillow: Cut the ruffle fabric into three 6″ × 45″ strips. Stitch them together into one long strip, then stitch the short ends right sides together to form a ring. Fold the joined strip in half right-side-out and sew gathering stitches along the raw edges. Pull the gathers up to fit around the pillow top.

Stitch the ends of the lace strip together to form a ring; gather the straight edge to match the fabric ruffle. Baste the lace and ruffle together. Stitch the ruffle unit, lace side down, to the embroidered pillow front, matching raw edges.

With right sides together, pin the backing fabric to the pillow front, ruffles sandwiched in between. Stitch around, leaving 10″ free along one edge. Turn right-side-out. Insert the pillow form and baste the opening closed. Knot a ribbon over each ring; sew the rings to the pillow center (marked with a star on the chart).

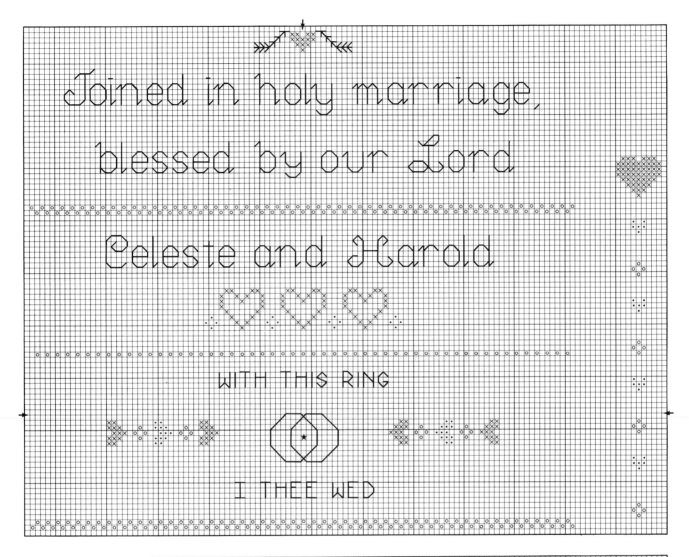

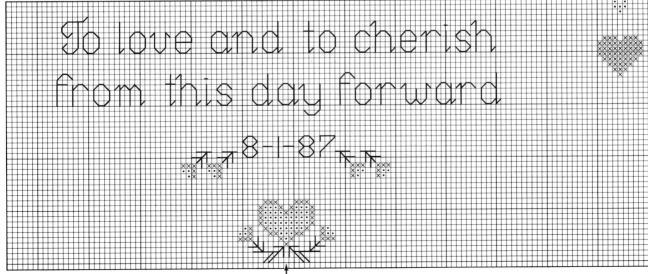

For I Am My Beloved's

A first-prize winner by Linda Scott Pietz
of Ontario, California

This piece truly captures the feeling of a traditional wedding
sampler design. But the designer elected to make a border of
her motto and give the names top billing—a reversal of the
usual placement. Linda Pietz worked on a needlepoint frame
to maintain the sizing in the needlepoint canvas, and when
she framed it for hanging she used a foam underpadding that
matches her sandy-brown background.

About Linda Scott Pietz

Linda Pietz was only 4 years old when two great-aunts
introduced her to the world of needlepoint. She began
designing much later, as a student at the Washington
University School of Arts in St. Louis. After graduation,
she started her own business designing and marketing hand-
painted needlepoint canvases to shops around the country.
More recently, she has also designed for two large
needlepoint manufacturers.

Linda's motto is from the Bible, a verse from the Song of
Solomon. "This motto beautifully expresses the commitment
and love between two people at their marriage."

The dog, by the way, is "the West Highland white terrier
that my husband and I bought to celebrate our engagement."

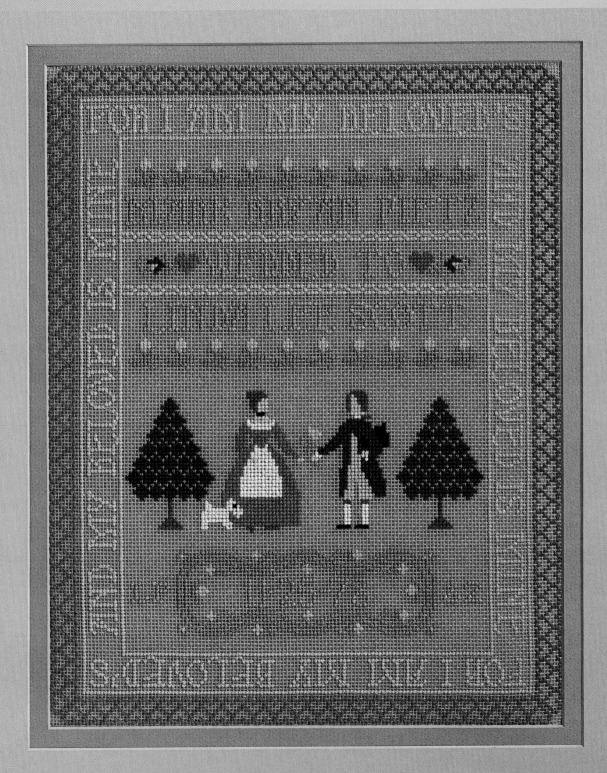

SIZE
Finished design area is 10½″ × 13½″

MATERIALS
14-mesh tan mono needlepoint canvas, cut 17″ × 20″
2 skeins deep rose embroidery floss
1 skein embroidery floss of other colors listed
Masking tape
Needlework frame

STITCH/COLOR KEYS

Cross-stitch

	Three strands	**DMC**	**Bates**
⟋	Rose—deep	3328	11
⊠	Blue—light	794	120
⊉	Royal blue	792	940
⊻	Beige	739	885
⑤	Cinnamon	355	5968
⊡	Emerald	702	239
◥	Green—dark	319	246
◣	Green—deep	890	879
◖	Yellow	743	297
△	Peach—pale	754	778
⊡	Ecru		
■	Black	310	403

PROCEDURE
Read General Directions, pages 205 to 214.
   Tape edges of canvas to prevent fraying. *Work canvas on a frame to keep mesh flat.* Work each cross-stich over intersection of canvas threads, as you would for needlepoint. Using additional letters and numbers, substitute names and date of your choice.
   Before framing, pad canvas with yellow foam or line to match canvas.

Additional Letters and Numbers

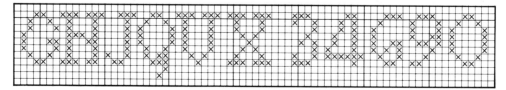

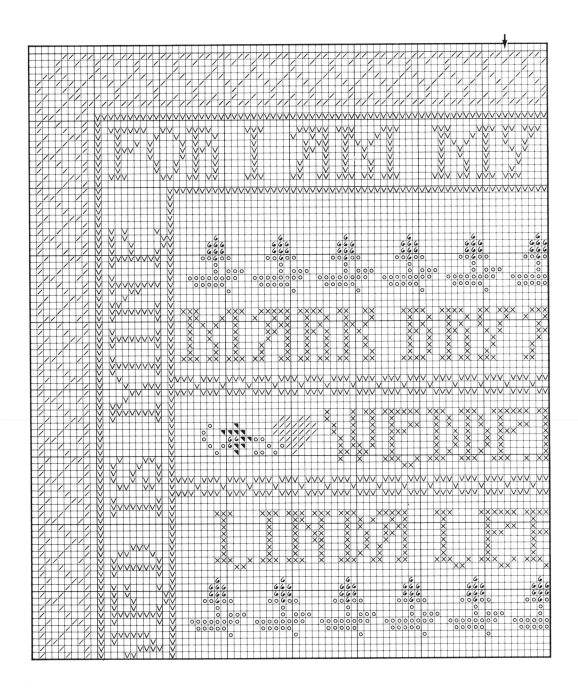

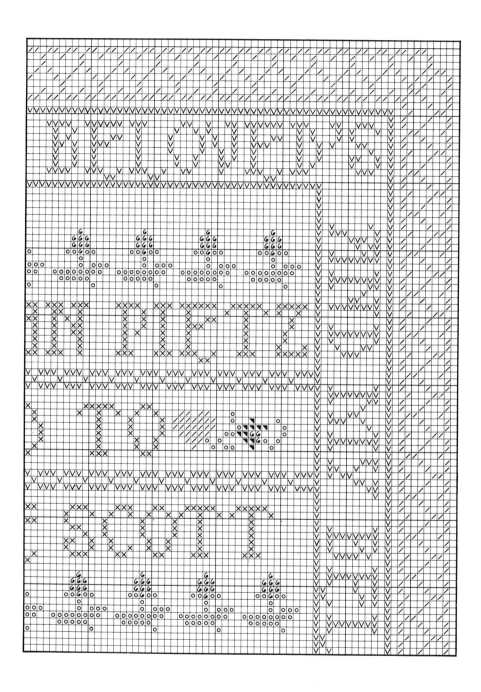

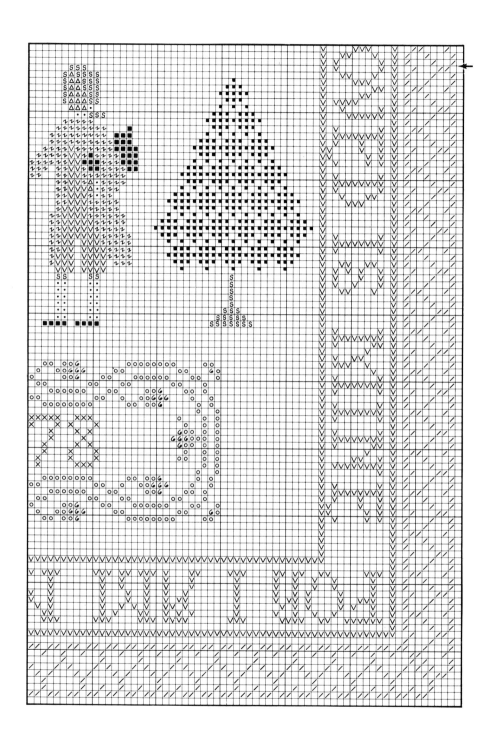

A Cat Makes
a House a Home

By Wendy A. Rarick of Dallas, Texas

Deceptively simple, this homey picture of two beribboned cats offers considerable challenge to the needleworker. The designer did a superb job of stitching the fireside pair in bold silhouettes, using half- and quarter-stitches all along those realistic curves, then outlining everything in backstitch. The cream Aida background softens the scene, and her unusual, professionally fashioned mat adds a touch of drama.

About Wendy A. Rarick

Wendy Rarick is originally from Milwaukee, Wisconsin, but she moved to Dallas about three-and-a-half years ago. The Raricks both work at Rockwell International—she in advertising and promotion with the communications division and her husband of two years as an electrical engineer.

Wendy enjoys many hobbies, though cross-stitch is her favorite. She also likes going to craft shows, working with animal-protection groups in her area, and "collecting anything that has to do with cats."

SIZE

Finished design area is 7″ × 9″

MATERIALS

14-count cream Aida cloth, cut 13″ × 15″
2 skeins deep rose embroidery floss

STITCH/COLOR KEYS

Cross-stitch

Two strands	DMC	Bates
☒ Deep rose	309	42

———— **Backstitch** (two strands): Deep rose

PROCEDURE

Read General Directions, pages 205 to 214.

Work all cross-stitches shown. Then work backstitches as smoothly as possible. Fill in small open areas within outlines with portions of cross-stitches.

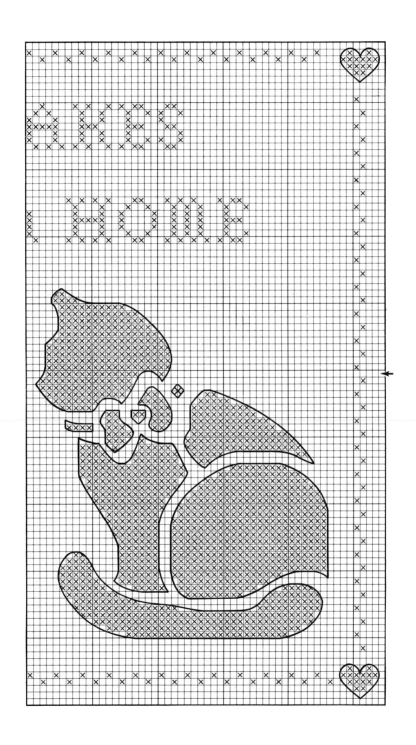

My Children Fill My Arms

By Nancy J. Reaves of Purcellville, Virginia

This cozy scene, with its warm message and cottage checkerboard border in two shades of blue, was designed to hang on the designer's kitchen wall. The bunny figures are modeled in shades of pink and brown and blue, which gives them a three-dimensional effect.

About Nancy J. Reaves

This sampler was inspired by Nancy Reaves's two children, Jason and Jasmine. She set out to capture the feelings she has "when I hold the two of them." Nancy lives with the children and her husband on a small farm in rural northern Virginia, where she enjoys reading, cooking, needlework, drawing, gardening, exploring the outdoors, and spending time with the family.

This is Nancy's first original cross-stitch design, but she has created many designs for other kinds of needlework, which she markets through Unique Creations, a small pattern company she owns with her sister-in-law.

My children fill my
arms with the
magic of their
presence,
and my heart
with love.
1987   NJJB

SIZE
Finished design area is 5³/₄″ × 8¹/₄″

MATERIALS
18-count white Aida cloth, cut 12″ × 15″
2 skeins slate blue embroidery floss
1 skein embroidery floss of other colors listed

STITCH/COLOR KEYS

Cross-stitch

	Two strands	DMC	Bates
⊞	Slate blue—light	932	920
⊘	Slate blue	931	921
⊙	Blue—light	775	128
▲	Navy	823	150
⊓	Beige	739	885
⊟	Tan	842	376
⚡	Brown—light	841	378
⊠	Brown	838	380
⊙	Green—light	368	240
⊡	Pink—pale	819	892
◔	Pink	776	24
◺	Yellow—pale	745	300
△	Yellow—light	744	301
P	Gold	725	306
■	Black	310	403
▽	White		

—————— **Backstitch** (two strands): Black

PROCEDURE
Read General Directions, pages 205 to 214.
Work cross-stitches where indicated, then work remaining stitches.

If of Thy Mortal Goods Thou Art Bereft . . .

A first-prize winner by Nancy Hillman Roberts
of Dugway, Utah

This impressive sampler is worked 18 stitches to the inch on one of the largest canvases in the contest: it measures 16″ × 20″. It took the designer the better part of a year to chart and execute her idea. The time she invested is evident in many beautiful details, such as the delicate frame cross-stitched with a single-thread around the motto, the small blossoms in the large alphabet, and the little ornaments on each side of the small alphabet. The designer has even incorporated her name in the border in a distinctive way.

About Nancy Hillman Roberts

Nancy Roberts took her motto from the "Garden of the Roses," written by a Persian poet named Sa'di (1184–1291). It is a favorite of hers and her sister's, and expresses her feeling that the most rewarding and precious things in her life have been "the intangible hyacinths that feed my soul, like being with my husband and family, my religion, working with the youth, and, yes, even quiet, reflecting hours doing needlework."

Nancy has experimented with many crafts, such as tole painting, stained glass, quilting, and ceramics, and has embroidered since her mother introduced her to needlework at about age 10. She first encountered counted cross-stitch a year after her college graduation, in a needlework shop in Copenhagen, Denmark. But she passed it up as "too difficult and beyond my talents." It was only after she had worked a

ABCDEFGHIJ
KLMNOPQRS
TUVWXYZ ⁘

IF OF THY MORTAL GOODS
THOU ART BEREFT
AND FROM THY SLENDER STORE
TWO LOAVES ALONE
TO THEE ARE LEFT
SELL ONE AND WITH THE DOLE
BUY HYACINTHS TO FEED THY SOUL

abcdefghijklmnopqrstuvwxyz 123456789

DESIGNED - STITCHED BY
NANCY HILLMAN ROBERTS

counted cross-stitch Mrs. Santa ornament, a free sample that came with another needlework purchase, that she found that counted cross-stitch was the perfect medium for her. She went straight from Mrs. Santa to designing this prize-winning sampler! Nancy plans to work her next design on hardanger, which she has grown to like while stitching some Danish counted-thread designs ordered from that Copenhagen shop.

Nancy teaches English at Dugway High School. Cross-stitch is a favorite tension-reliever and creative outlet.

SIZE
Finished design area is 16″ × 20″

MATERIALS
18-count white Aida cloth, cut 22″ × 26″
2 skeins embroidery floss each, light pink and lavender
1 skein embroidery floss of other colors listed

STITCH/COLOR KEYS

Cross-stitch

	Two strands	DMC	Bates
☑	Blue—light	809	130
▲	Navy	820	134
⊡	Pink—light	605	50
◖	Pink—dark	603	76
◿	Lavender	210	104
◎	Purple	552	101
	Purple—dark	550	102 (backstitch only)
◲	Green—light	368	240
△	Green	367	216
◉	Green—dark	319	246
⅃	Emerald—light	913	209
☒	Fuchsia	718	88
	Fuchsia—dark	915	89 (backstitch only)
⊓	Yellow—light	445	288
⑤	Yellow—bright	444	291
⊟	Coral—pale	948	778
	Coral—light	353	8 (backstitch only)
◿	Coral	352	10
◵	Brown—light	436	363
⋋	Brown—dark	801	357
	Brown—deep	938	381 (backstitch only)

——— **Backstitch** (one strand)

Chart 1, zigzag stripes:

   Outer line A: Dark brown
   Inner line B: Coral
   Center line C: Light coral

Use darker shades of matching colors on all remaining outlines except for large hyacinths (see below).

Chart 4, large hyacinths: Lower left flower is same color as lower right. For center flower, substitute lavender for light pink, purple for dark pink. **Backstitch:** *Pink flowers:* Outline dark pink areas, yellow spots and right edge of flower with fuchsia, left edge with dark pink. *Purple flower:* Outline purple areas, yellow spots and right edge with dark purple, left edge with purple.

PROCEDURE

Read General Directions, pages 205 to 214.

Work Chart 1, being sure that lines from arrows cross at center of fabric. (*Note:* Chart 1 is not centered vertically.) *Work the dark green border stitches with 1 strand floss.*

Work Chart 2 (half shown) above Chart 1, leaving a 6-stitch space. Repeat Chart 2 across, omitting center stitch (arrows).

Work Chart 3 alphabet above Chart 2, leaving a 4-stitch space.

Matching top center arrow of Chart 3 to bottom arrow of border and leaving a 4-stitch space, work border in upper right corner. (Match A to A and B to B on border sections.) Repeat border in upper left corner, omitting center stitch (arrows). Continue border along sides of sampler to lower edge of Chart 1, working hyacinths in desired colors.

Work Chart 4 in lower right corner, matching border at broken line (D), using additional letters to fill in your name. Repeat Chart 4 in lower left corner, placing border on left side and omitting lettering. Repeat hyacinth (purple) in center.

Additional Letters

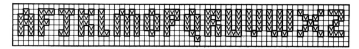

CENTER LEFT   CHART 1

CHART 1

CENTER MIDDLE

CHART 1   CENTER RIGHT

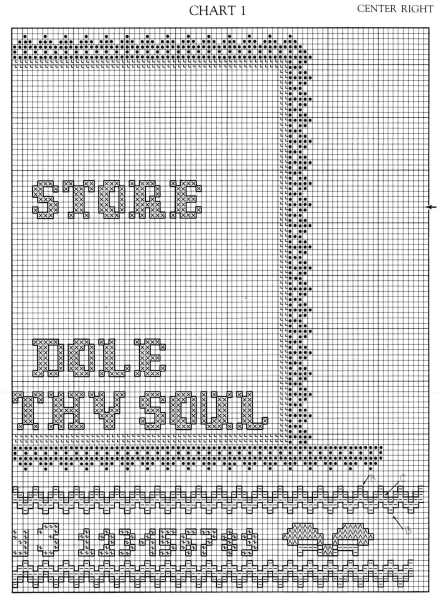

CENTER MOTIF   CHART 2

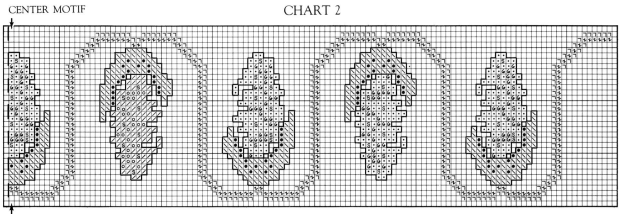

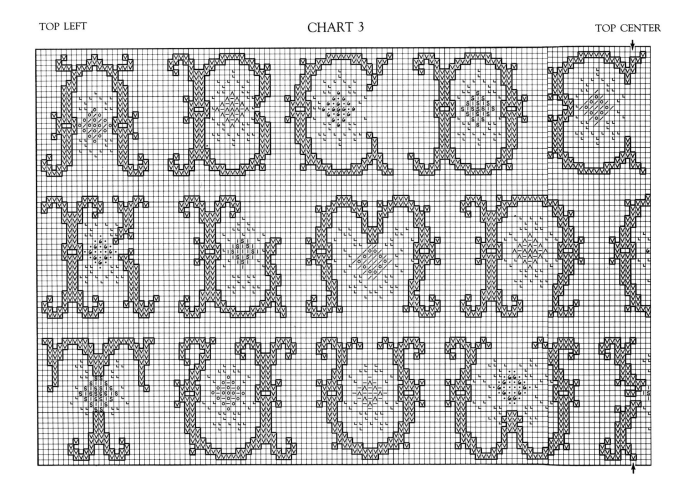

TOP CENTER

CHART 3

TOP RIGHT

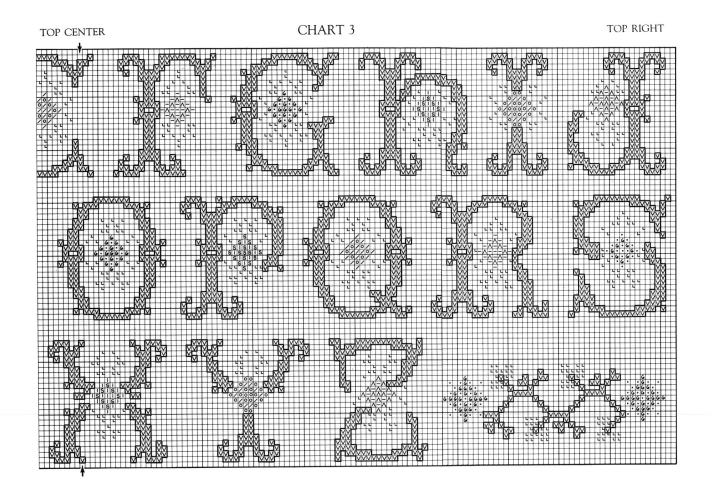

CHART 4

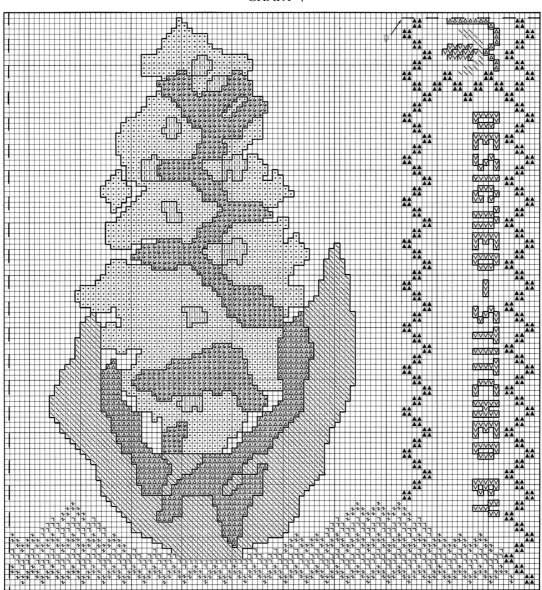

BOTTOM MOTIF

BORDER

For Unto You
Is Born This Day . . .

By Rose Saladis of Seattle, Washington

Fresh in concept, pleasingly balanced, and harking back to
the age-old, long-loved symbols of Christmas, this is a
sampler many cross-stitchers would take pleasure in making.
It is all in cross-stitch except for the outlines and Scripture
verse, which are done in backstitch. The designer recognized
that incorporating the many things that she associates with
Christmas was leading to a rather busy design, and she
decided to keep her colors largely to red, green, and gold.

About Rose Saladis

When Rose Saladis read about the "Expressions of Love"
contest, her first thought was of Jesus and His birth, and she
decided to build a design "around that expression
of love."

    This is Rose's first original sampler, although she has done
embroidery, crewel, and needlework for many years, and
cross-stitch for the last two. Her winning sampler took her
about two weeks from beginning the design to the last stitch
completed. She is keeping the sampler as part of the Saladis
family Christmas decorations: "Each year I'll put it up for the
month of December."

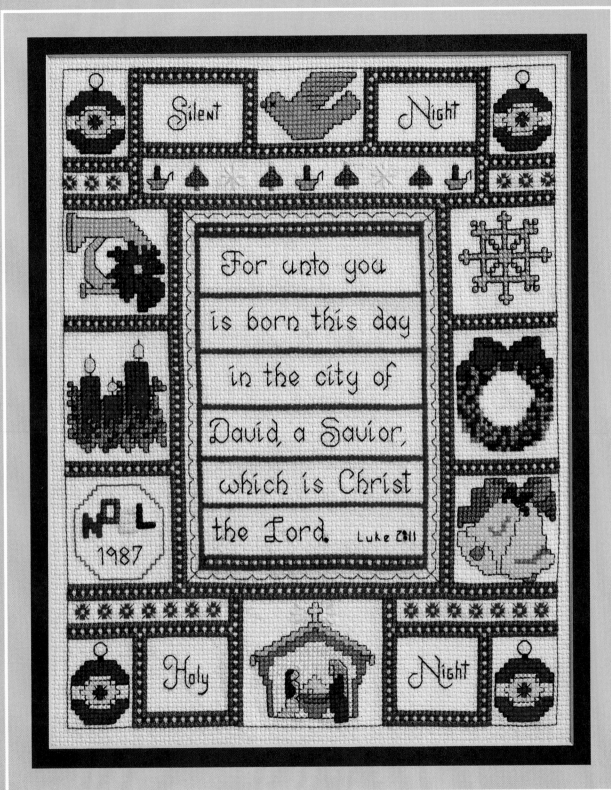

SIZE
Finished design area is 8″ × 10″

MATERIALS
14-count white Aida cloth, cut 14″ × 16″
1 skein embroidery floss of each color listed

STITCH/COLOR KEYS

Cross-stitch

	Two strands	DMC	Bates
◹	Pink	899	27
⊠	Red	666	46
▼	Red—dark	304	47
◢	Cranberry	498	20
◔	Green—bright	906	256
◉	Christmas green	700	229
▲	Green—dark	895	246
◿	Yellow	307	289
⊟	Yellow—dark	726	295
⊻	Gold	729	890
⫿	Blue—pale	775	128
◣	Royal blue	796	133
⊟	Peach—pale	754	778
◪	Brown—light	782	308
◪	Gray—light	415	398
■	Black	310	403
⊡	White		

——— **Backstitch** (one strand)
    Lines A: Red
    Line B: Christmas green
    Rays (C): Dark yellow
    Use black for all remaining outlines.

PROCEDURE
Read General Directions, pages 205 to 214.
    Work cross-stitches where indicated, then work remaining stitches.

Silent Night

For unto you
is born this day
in the city of
David a Savior
which is Christ
the Lord. Luke 2:11

1987

Holy Night

Plant a Memory Garden

A second-prize winner by Robyn Schaap and Danette Wright of Salt Lake City, Utah

This tribute takes its composition from the garden plots and old-time quilts that the designers associate with their grandfather. To achieve a soft, subtle effect, they chose Fiddler's cloth for its homespun feeling and selected mostly muted colors, spiced with touches of salmon. The light, pretty border, outlined with running stitches, is given textural interest by the skillful combination of half cross-stitches and single-thread and double-thread cross-stitches in the patches of plaid. Finally, the designers enhanced their work with a double mat, a dense, dark blue over a lighter blue that matches the houses in the border.

About Robyn Schaap and Danette Wright

Robyn Schaap and Danette Wright are sisters who have worked together on many creative projects. Robyn works full-time in New York City, while Danette combines part-time work with caring for her two children in Salt Lake City.

Both sisters declared they were too busy to enter the contest when their mother suggested they might. They later changed their minds and worked on the piece secretly, planning it as a surprise gift for their mother. Their motto is taken from a poem written by their grandfather.

PLANT A
MEMORY
GARDEN

IN MEMORY OF OUR GRANDPA, M. EARL MARSHALL
BY DANETTE E. WRIGHT & ROBYN E. SCHAAP 1987

SIZE
Finished design area is 9³/₄″ × 11″

MATERIALS
14-count tweed Fiddler's cloth or Aida cloth, cut 16″ × 17″
1 skein embroidery floss of each color listed

STITCH/COLOR KEYS

Cross-stitch

	Two strands	DMC	Bates
⊞	Blue—light	3325	159
⦿	Sky blue	334	145
⊠	Blue—dark	311	149
☑	Salmon	760	9
◕	Salmon—dark	3328	11
◪	Sea green	993	186
▲	Emerald	909	229
⊡	Mauve—light	3042	869
⋈	Mauve	3041	871
⊙	Yellow	744	301

- - - - - **Running stitch** (two strands): Dark blue

───── **Backstitch** (one strand): Dark blue

Plaid blocks: Work vertical dark salmon stripes (A) with one strand. Work light mauve stripes in half cross-stitch (except at intersections), working stitches on vertical stripes from upper right corner to lower left and stitches on horizontal stripes from upper left corner to lower right.

PROCEDURE
Read General Directions, pages 205 to 214.

Work cross-stitches, half cross-stitches, and running stitches. Work backstitches, substituting names and date of your choice.

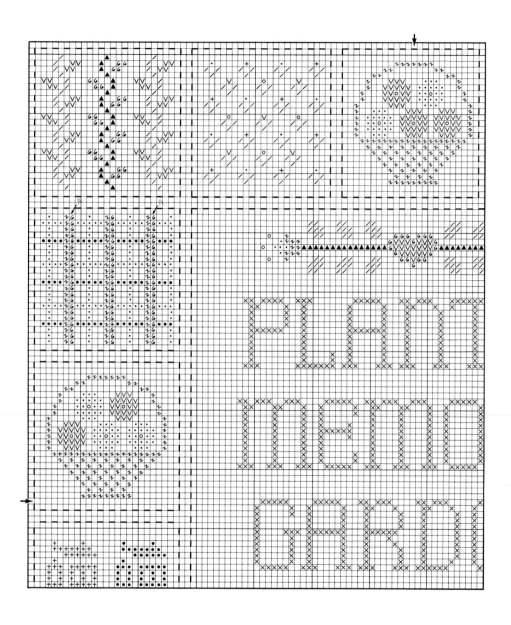

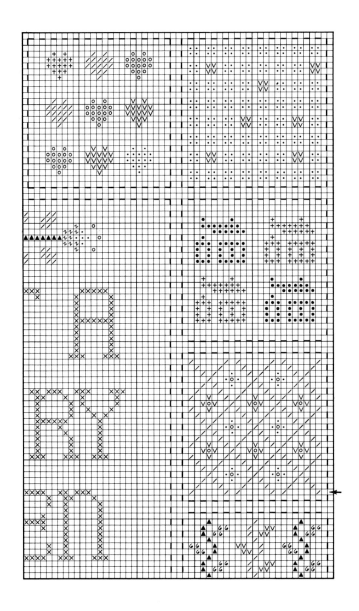

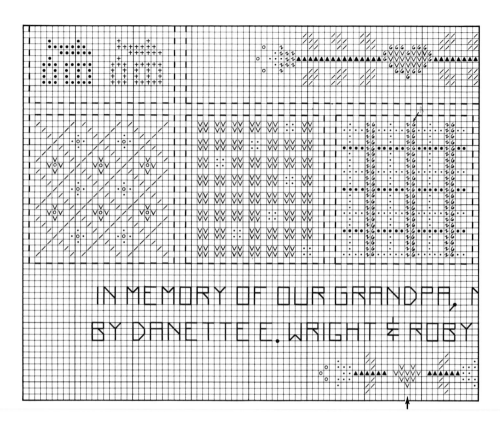

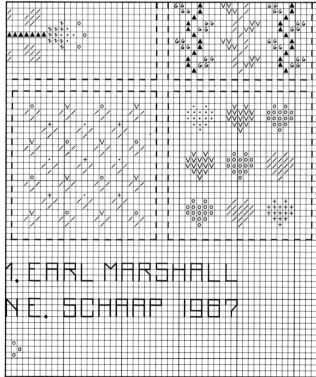

One in Joy, One in Sorrow

By Lin Vickery of Latham, New York

A charming picture-postcard of a sampler, this farmyard scene should inspire many cross-stitch designers. It is true folk art, with everything in its symmetrical place, from the sun and the cloud, and the trees so neatly paired, to the man and the woman sharing the heart. The backstitched motto adds just the right ingenuous touch.

About Lin Vickery

Lin Vickery describes herself as "a fully committed mother-at-home, devoted to the care and nurturing of my family. We have three children, ages 13, 12, and 1½, and are in our third year of home schooling. My greatest satisfaction comes from teaching both values and skills to our children, and I consider this work to be my most valuable contribution to the world, because I am convinced that strong families make a strong society."

Lin loves to cook from scratch. She bakes the family's bread and tends a large vegetable garden during the summer months. She teaches several private piano students from September to June.

Lin came upon the contest on her sixteenth wedding anniversary. "Having just completed our school year at home, I was ripe for a creative challenge." Three weeks went into the pattern, five weeks into the stitching ("a kind of cross-stitch marathon for me"). She had designed samplers in the past, but this was to be her first picture. She knew she wanted a quaint farmhouse and yard, but what to put in the yard? She let her older children help decide which animals to include. Then she spent weeks pondering over the motto.

Would it communicate what she wanted to say? She finished the picture before making up her mind. Then, could she fit the motto she chose into the space at the top? Yes, if she slanted the words into the space that remained! The results are fresh, humorous, and delightfully personal.

Although Lin originally designed the sampler for the contest, it is a gift to her husband. She thought of hanging it in their bedroom, "because it seems so personal," but her husband has "insisted that it be hung where everyone who enters our home will see it."

SIZE
Finished design area is 6¼" × 10"

MATERIALS
14-count cream Aida cloth, cut 12" × 16"
2 skeins embroidery floss each, cream, light green, and pale green
1 skein embroidery floss of other colors listed

STITCH/COLOR KEYS

Cross-stitch

	Two strands	DMC	Bates
⌐	Green—pale	369	213
⌐	Green—light	320	216
◼	Green	367	216
⊙	Green—dark	319	246
⊟	Pink—light	3326	25
△	Pink	335	42
◺	Red—light	3705	35
◹	Red	326	59
◿	Blue—light	794	120
◥	Blue	799	130
⊙	Gray—light	648	900
⊠	Slate gray	317	400
⊞	Yellow	727	293
◖	Salmon	352	10
▯	Peach—pale	951	366
⋁	Tan	841	378
▲	Brown—dark	839	38
⋅	White		
	Cream	712	387

———— **Backstitch** (two strands)
    Border vine: Light green (one strand)
    Border stamens: Yellow
    Tree outlines: Dark green
    House and details: Slate gray
    Sun's rays: Yellow
    Use dark brown for all remaining backstitching.

● **French knots** (one strand)
    Flowers A: Pink (*Note:* Work single yellow stitch in petals.)
    Flowers B: Yellow (*Note:* Work single yellow stitch in petals.)
    Stamen tips (C): Yellow
    Eyes (people and animals): Dark brown

Straight stitch (one strand)
    Ducks' bills: single straight stitch in salmon

PROCEDURE

Read General Directions, pages 205 to 214.

Line D separates sky and mountains. Do not work stitching on line.

Work all cross-stitches shown. Work sky, mountains, and grass in cross-stitch in colors indicated. Work all backstitches. Fill tiny open areas within outlines with portions of cross-stitches.

Children Play the Harmony

A second-prize winner by Lorraine J. Wixom of Ogden, Utah

This sampler could be the title page for a collection of delightful fairy tales. Its pictorial quality is enhanced by the designer's embroidery techniques. She worked on 32-count linen, stitching over two threads of the fabric, and using one strand of embroidery thread throughout. The rosebuds in the initial letters and the tendrils that spring from the vines in her sampler are especially graceful touches.

About Lorraine J. Wixom

Lorraine Wixom's uplifting sentiment comes from the 19th-century hymn "Love at Home," a Mormon favorite that her mother taught her when she was very young. In her sampler she wanted to recognize the two great loves of her life: her family and music. She views them almost as one. "Just as a melody is supported and given depth and beauty by its accompaniment, I feel my life has been broadened and beautified by the lives of my children."

The frame of her piece incorporates the words of the hymn, and each toy and instrument represents one or more of her children. Her daughter loves to collect bears, for example, and her oldest son plays the trumpet. "My youngest son has loved trains since he was tiny, and my second son created wonderful planes and spaceships from plastic building blocks."

Lorraine has given away most of her counted cross-stitch pieces, but plans to keep this particular sampler to display with pride in her home.

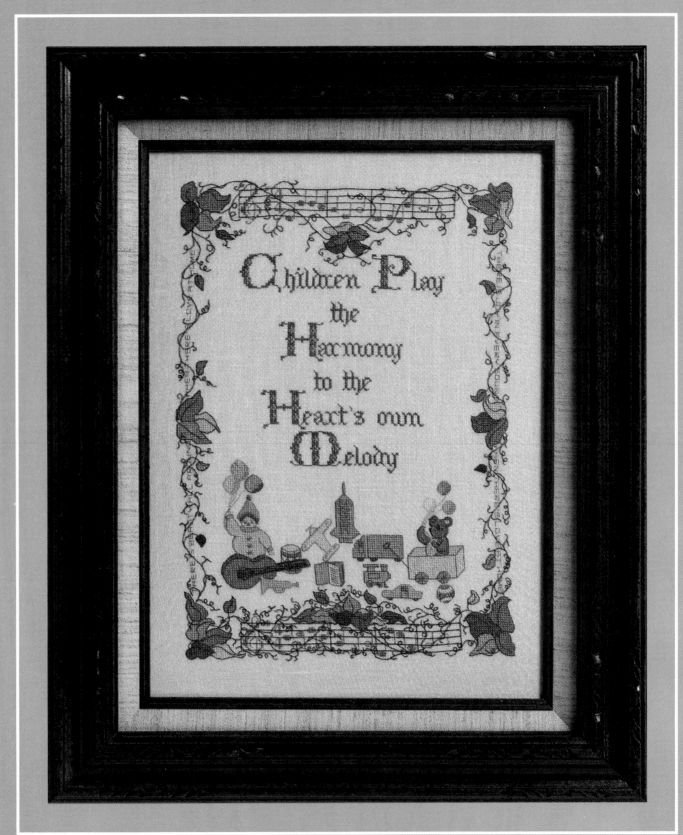

SIZE

Finished design area is 9³/4″ × 13″

MATERIALS

32-count (average) even-weave linen, cut 18″ × 21″
1 skein embroidery floss of each color listed

STITCH/COLOR KEYS

Cross-stitch

One strand	DMC	Bates
⊡ Green—pale	3348	265
◎ Green—light	3347	266
⊠ Green	3346	257
◖ Green—dark	3345	268
▲ Green—deep	895	246
�𝌆 Pink—light	3326	25
◸ Pink	335	42
◺ Peach	754	778
◹ Tan	738	942
◩ Cocoa	434	309
Ⓢ Chocolate	433	371
◿ Gray—pale	762	397
⊞ Gray	415	398
Gray—dark	317	400 (backstitch only)
◩ Taupe	646	8581
⊟ Blue—pale	747	158
◸ Blue—light	519	167
◺ Wedgwood blue	794	120
⭡ Aqua	598	167
◉ Teal green	926	779
◰ Gold—pale	677	886
⊟ Gold	783	307
⊡ White		

—————— **Backstitch** (one strand)
      Vines and leaf outlines: Deep green
      Book and engine: Wedgwood blue
      Guitar strings: Chocolate
      Use darker shades of matching colors for all remaining toy
        outlines.
      Border letters: Pink
      Musical notes: Taupe
      Staffs: Dark gray
      Balloon strings B: Gold
      Balloon strings C: Light blue

✳ **Smyrna cross-stitch** (one strand): Pink (on clown)

PROCEDURE
Read General Directions, pages 205 to 214.

Work all cross-stitches over 2 threads. Work remaining stitches.

Note: Work cross-stitches with cocoa in Area A on guitar before working strings. Work single pink vertical stitch over pink cross-stitch on flowers (D), to add texture.

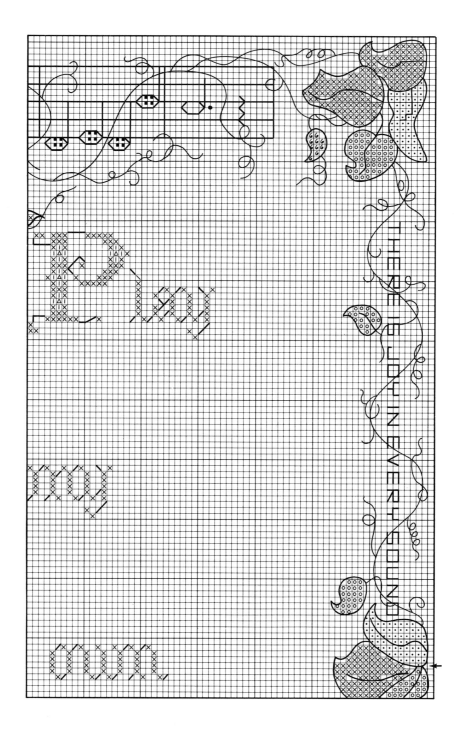

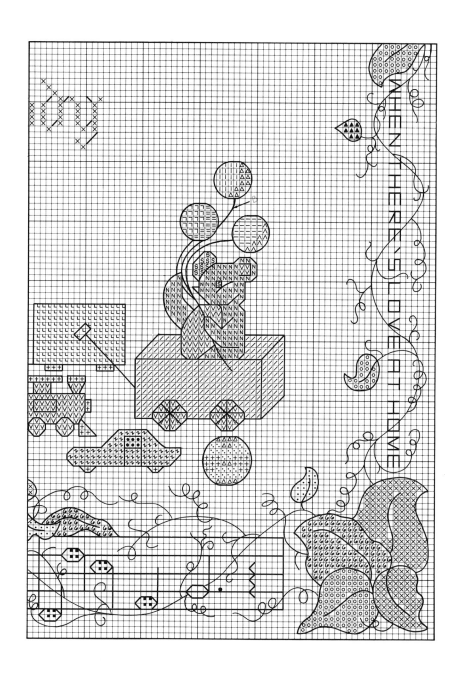

General Directions

The Materials

FABRIC

All of the fabrics for the samplers in this book, with one exception, are even-weave Aida cloth or linen. Every even-wave fabric has the same number of threads woven vertically and horizontally per square inch.

Aida cloth is woven in tiny squares, which are easy to count. It is especially made for cross-stitch. You work one cross-stitch over each square. On linen, work one cross-stitch over two threads vertically and horizontally (unless otherwise specified). If you are using 14-count Aida cloth (14 squares per inch), you will have 14 stitches per inch. If you are using 26-count linen (26 threads per inch), you will have 13 stitches per inch.

Both fabrics are available in needlework shops everywhere.

If you decide to use a fabric with a different count than the one specified, your sampler will be a different size. A fabric with a higher count will produce a smaller sampler (more stitches per inch). A lower count will produce a larger sampler (fewer stitches per inch).

FLOSS

These designs were all worked with DMC 6-strand embroidery floss, which is widely available. You can, however, substitute Susan Bates Anchor floss if you wish. We give the color numbers for both DMC and Bates. Some of the Bates colors are not an exact match for the DMC, but they are very close and make suitable alternatives. If you are using Bates floss, you will find that occasionally two close shades are listed with the same number. Simply use the same shade in both areas of the sampler.

Cut your floss into 18″ lengths. Separate the strands and use the number specified.

In order to keep your colors neatly separated and ready for use, you might make a simple thread holder. Cut a piece of cardboard about 4″ deep and long enough to mark on it the same number of dots as there are colors, spacing the dots 1″ apart. Punch or cut a ¼″-diameter hole at each dot. Write the color and number over each hole, then draw the 18″ lengths of floss through the holes.

NEEDLES

Use a blunt tapestry needle, which passes easily between the threads of the fabric and does not pierce the fabric itself. Needle numbers 24 or 26 will work well with our fabrics. The higher the number, the finer the needle.

HOOP OR FRAME

Aida cloth is sturdy enough to hold its shape without a hoop, but a hoop is generally desirable for linen. If you enjoy working on a frame, you may use one for either fabric.

The Basics

PREPARING FABRIC

Trim your fabric to at least 3″ larger on all sides than the finished design area. Whipstitch the raw edges with sewing thread to keep them from fraying.

CHARTS

Many of the charts are separated into two or more sections in order to fit them into the book. The best way to prepare your chart so that you can follow it easily is to photocopy the sections and tape them together with clear tape.

Each symbol on the chart represents one stitch worked in a certain color. Near the chart you will find a color key specifying the colors, their numbers in DMC and Bates floss and the color symbols to match to the chart.

CENTERING THE DESIGN

Fold your fabric in half crosswise and lengthwise. Then insert a pin at the point of the folded corner and open out the fabric. You will find that the pin is at the center of the fabric.

To locate the center of your chart, use a ruler and colored pencil to connect the side arrows, and then connect the top and bottom arrows. The two lines will cross at the chart's center.

BEGINNING TO STITCH

It is best to start at the center of the fabric so that the design will be positioned properly. On some charts you will not find a stitch at the exact center; in this case simply count the squares of Aida cloth or the threads of linen to the nearest stitch and start there.

Never knot your thread; secure the ends on the back of the fabric either by weaving the thread for ½″ or so through the stitches or by holding down a short tail on the back and working over it.

The color may show through if you carry your thread across an empty area on the back. To avoid this, cut your thread, bury the ends, and start again.

Always work each stitch in two operations: Bring the needle down through the fabric and draw the thread through; then bring the needle up through the fabric and draw the thread through. You will find that your stitches lie flatter than they would if you pushed your needle in and out in one motion as for sewing.

PROCEDURE

The designs shown here are worked primarily in cross-stitch, but many of the motifs are outlined in backstitch, and a number of poems, quotations, signatures and dates are worked in backstitch as well. On a few of the designs, still other embroidery stitches have been added. In most cases, work all the cross-stitches first, and then the backstitches. Finish with any other stitches required. (*Note:* The one exception is the *I Love to Knit* sampler; follow the special instructions for that design.)

ALPHABETS AND NUMBERS

Letters and numbers have been provided for certain designs to help you personalize your samplers by substituting names and dates of your choice. We have not given the whole alphabet or all the numbers (1–10), because you can find the missing ones within the design. The samplers for which additional letters or number have not been supplied are simple enough that you should have no trouble making substitutions. Use a sheet of graph paper to work out your names and dates.

FINISHING

You should not have to block cross-stitch worked on even-weave fabric. If your sampler is not soiled and just needs pressing, lay it facedown on a padded board, spread a damp cloth over it and press.

If your work is soiled, hand-wash it in a mild soap solution and cool water. Rinse well and press. It might be wise to check the colorfastness of the floss first by washing scraps with a piece of leftover fabric.

Framing. You have put a lot of work, love and patience into your sampler, and we recommend that you have it mounted and framed professionally. But if you would like to frame it yourself, here's one method: Purchase a frame and mat (if desired) that will allow about 1″ of fabric to show beyond the border of the finished design. Cut a piece of cardboard to fit the frame (not too tightly: you must allow room for the fabric). Cut a piece of backing fabric the same color and size as the embroidered fabric. If you are not using a mat and you would like padding, cut a piece of thin quilt batting or foam slightly smaller than the cardboard. Lightly glue the padding to the cardboard. Center and stretch the backing and embroidery over the padding, folding the raw edges to the wrong side. Staple or tape with masking tape. Insert your sampler into the frame.

The Stitches

CROSS-STITCH

Make a row of stitches, each slanting diagonally over either one square of Aida cloth or two threads horizontally and vertically of linen. Each stitch forms half of one cross-stitch. Work back over these stitches, making diagonal stitches in the opposite direction and always inserting your needle in the same holes. All stitches must cross in the same direction (unless a deliberate decision is made to add to the texture of the design by breaking this rule).

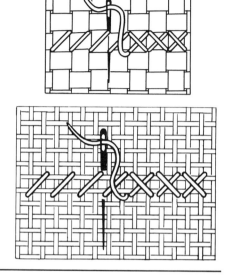

BACKSTITCH

Bring your needle up at A, down at B, up at C, down at A, up at D, down at C, up at E, down at D, up at F, down at E, up at G, down at F, up at H, down at G. Continue as shown. Your stitches will be twice as long on the back as on the front. When working on Aida cloth, work each stitch over a square; on linen, work each stitch over two threads.

FILL-IN CROSS-STITCHES

When working a backstitch outline around a cross-stitch motif, you will often have tiny sections at the edges of the motif that will not accommodate a full cross-stitch. (Many of these areas on the charts are too small to have color symbols.) To fill in the ragged edges, you must work portions of cross-stitches. These portions of cross-stitches are shown shaded on the Diagonal Outline and Shaped Outline diagrams.

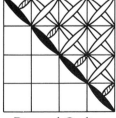

Diagonal Outline

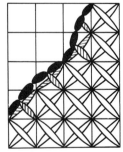

Shaped Outline

CHAIN STITCH

Bring your needle to the right side of the fabric. Hold the thread down with your thumb. Insert the needle as close as possible to the spot where the thread emerges and bring it out the desired distance away, catching the loop of thread on the front of the fabric. Draw needle through loop. Continue making chains.

CHAIN STITCH (OPEN)

Bring your needle up at A. Hold the thread down with your thumb; insert the needle at B. Bring it to the front again a little below A and draw the thread through over the thread loop. Leave the first loop formed a little loose so that the next stitch can be easily inserted in it. Continue as shown.

COUCHING

Place the ribbon or thread to be couched along the line being covered. Hold it down with your thumb. With thread, work small stitches over the ribbon to hold it in place, always bringing the needle up on the same side of the ribbon and inserting it on the other. Space your stitches about $1/2''$ apart.

CROSS-STITCH OVER CROSS-STITCH

Using one color, work a row of cross-stitches over 4-block squares of Aida cloth. Then, using another color, work a second row of cross-stitches over the first row, as shown.

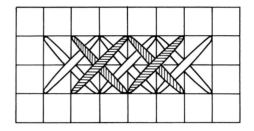

FLY STITCH

Bring your needle up at the top left of the stitch (A). Insert the needle exactly opposite (B), leaving a slightly loose loop, and bring the needle out at a point C centered below A and B, catching the loop. Draw the thread through. Make a small stitch to tie down loop.

FRENCH KNOT

Bring your needle up at the place where knot is to be made (A). Wind the thread one or two times around the point of the needle as shown. Insert the needle into the fabric as close as possible (B) to the spot where the thread emerged (but not in the exact spot), and pull it to the wrong side, holding the twists in place.

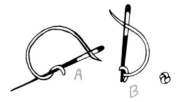

HALF CROSS-STITCH

Simply work the first half of a cross-stitch over an Aida cloth square or over one linen thread. (*Note:* Working over one linen thread is the same as working needlepoint on a mesh background.)

HERRINGBONE STITCH

Bring your needle up at A, down at B, up at C, down at D, up at E. Continue across the row, as shown.

MONTENEGRIN CROSS-STITCH

Work over a row of Aida cloth squares. *Diagram 1:* Bring your needle up at A, down at B (upper right corner of next square), up at C, down at D. *Diagram 2:* Bring the needle up at C again and then down at E to make a vertical stitch. Repeat this procedure across the row (*Diagram 3*).

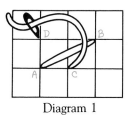 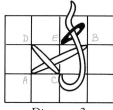

Diagram 1   Diagram 2

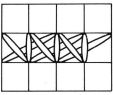

Diagram 3

PLAIT STITCH

Make diagonal stitches, working one forward and then one backward, as follows: Bring needle up at A, down at B, up at C, down at D, up at E, down at F, up at G, down at B, up at C, down at H, up at I, down at F. Repeat this procedure across the row.

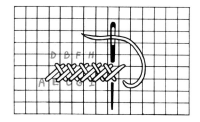

RICE STITCH

Make a cross-stitch over one square of Aida cloth. Then work a tiny straight stitch diagonally across the corner over each arm of the cross.

ROCOCO STITCH

Work over a 4-block square of Aida cloth. *Diagram 1:* Bring your needle up at A, down at B, up at C, down at D. Working in the same holes, make another A–B stitch and hold it to the left of the first. Cross it at its center as for C–D before. Make two more A–B stitches to the right of the first one, crossing each at its center (*Diagram 2*).

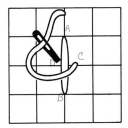
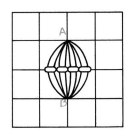

Diagram 1   Diagram 2

RUNNING STITCH

Work from right to left as shown, working each stitch over every other square of Aida cloth.

SATIN STITCH

Bring your needle up at one edge of area to be covered and then insert the needle at the opposite edge. Pull the thread through, making sure the stitch lies flat over the area to be covered without puckering the fabric. Return to the starting line by carrying the thread underneath the fabric. Make your stitches as close together as possible to fill the area completely.

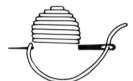

SMYRNA CROSS

Work over one square of Aida cloth. Make a cross-stitch, then work first a horizontal stitch and then a vertical stitch over it.

STAR STITCH

Work over one square of Aida cloth. Bring needle up at A, down in center of square, up at B, down in center. Continue around square as shown.

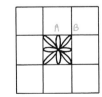

Index

All of us at Sedgewood® Press are dedicated to offering you, our customer, the best books we can create. We are particularly concerned that all of the instructions for making the projects are clear and accurate. We welcome your comments and would like to hear any suggestions you may have. Please address your correspondence to Customer Service Department, Sedgewood® Press, Meredith Corporation, 750 Third Avenue, New York, NY 10017.

For information on how you can have *Better Homes and Gardens* delivered to your door, write to: Mr. Robert Austin, P.O. Box 4536, Des Moines, IA 50336.